THE
COMPLETE
BOOK OF
INSURANCE
Protecting Your

LIFE, HEALTH, PROPERTY & INCOME

BEN G. BALDWIN

PROBUS PUBLISHING COMPANY
Chicago, Illinois

ISBN 1-55738-079-1

Printed in the United States of America

2   3   4   5   6   7   8   9   0

CONTENTS

PREFACE

A major portion of everyone's budget goes to paying for various forms of insurance. Some of those dollars are spent wisely, some are wasted—the trick is in knowing which is which. Insurance seems to pose problems not only for buyers, but also for professional advisors. The International Association for Financial Planning conducted a survey, which found that personal risk management was the area of financial planning that gave the professionals the greatest difficulty. If they find it tough, it is likely that you will, too. The purpose of this book is to eliminate the mystique that surrounds insurance and makes it seem incomprehensible. I hope to make the insurance decisions you face in your daily life not only comprehensible, but actually easy!

This book originated with my asking my insurance clients questions and listening to their answers: a process once called "needs selling," which has evolved into a part of what is today called financial planning. Whether financial planning appeals to you or not depends on your personal experience with those who practice it, and whether they pursue it in your best interests, or in their own. It makes sense to buy for *your* reasons, not those of the salesperson. The world of insurance and financial products is filled with salespeople who want to sell you the latest "hot product" for one reason—to make the sale. Unfortunately, you often let them. This book will help you match your insurance needs with products that will satisfy them.

A major milestone in the development of this book occurred when a Chicago investor by the name of Angelo Geocaris came to the author in 1981 and said that he wanted to build "the McDonalds" of personal financial planning, a free-standing financial planning center where people could obtain a quality, objective, financial plan at a reasonable cost. While the Financial Security Centre was in full operation, manufacturing financial plans, the author would find himself with half a dozen plans all opened to the risk management and insurance section. With cassette recorder in hand, he would go from plan to plan dictating recommendations for each client for disability insurance, medical insurance, home, auto and liability insurance, life insurance and annuities . . . repeating himself time after time: in effect, writing a book on insurance for each individual client. Each "book" had a great many things in common. I found that much of what I wanted for each client was what I wanted for myself, and what I want for you.

The next step in the development of this book was to begin teaching credible financial planners (not the phonies, who already know what they want to sell you) how to build the personal risk management section—the defensive section—of a financial plan. This culminated in a course written for the California Society of Certified Public Accountants which has been adopted nationally by the American Society of Certified Public Accountants. The course, "Risk Management and Insurance in Personal Financial Planning," is used as part of their Certificate of Educational Achievement Program in Personal Financial Planning. Since it was published in 1988, it has been taught to hundreds of CPAs around the country. This author has had the opportunity to teach it many times. During the sessions many CPAs asked me to present it in book form, intended for their clients. The CPAs could do a better job and charge less for a financial plan when working with a well-informed client.

This, then, is that book. This is the "defensive section" of your financial plan. It won't make you rich: it is designed to help you avoid becoming poor. This book will help you deal with the professional, client-oriented insurance salespeople, and to distinguish them from "sell anything" salespeople who care more about their own needs than yours.

This book will help you solve the policy puzzle. It will help you select policies and spend your insurance dollars wisely. You will learn how to be a winner by not being a loser.

One of the unique features of this book is its "Action Letters." Once you have read about a particular type of coverage, you will find that the author has written a letter to your insurance professional for you specifying what you want and need. Of course, you will change and adapt these letters to suit your own needs, but you will find it much easier to do so than to create your own. You will find "Action Letters" for disability insurance, private health insurance, employer provided medical insurance, nursing home insurance, life insurance and home, auto and liability insurance and annuities.

The author of this book is an admitted designation collector. He is a CLU, CFP, ChFC, MSM and MSFS. He has been either taking or teaching classes on finance and insurance since 1964. He has taught the full curriculum for the Certified Financial Planning designation twice and has taught the Chartered Life Underwriter (CLU) courses and the Chartered Financial Consultant (ChFC) courses to many insurance professionals. He has taught more CPAs to understand insurance than any other insurance professional.

The Complete Book of Insurance: How to Protect Life, Health, Property and Income, is the culmination of all the efforts of an author who has spent 60 percent of his time selling insurance products, 20 percent learning about them, and 20 percent teaching about them.

Acknowledgements

This book is dedicated to my support group. No one walks alone; I am blessed with a teammate and facilitator, my wife Moses, my chief editor and critic, without whom I would get nothing done. In fact, without her I would not have the rest of my support group, editors and critics—sons B.G., Peter (and his wife Susan Gough Baldwin), and Michael; and my daughter and business associate, Katie (and her husband, Doug Leipprandt). They all work very hard to keep me on track. Even Mike's fiancé, Katie Barg, a professional editor, went over this book and offered suggestions and corrections to make it more understandable.

Katie and Moses kept the office going, while Leslie Murphy made the word processor hum at the same time that she was editing and offering helpful suggestions.

Of course, none of this would have come about had not Bill Kaun, CPA, invited me to speak before the American Institute of Certified Public Accountants' first Personal Financial Planning Conference in 1984, and had not Jim Wilson, CPA, the conference chairman, become my mentor thereafter.

I also must thank my clients, who have been forced to be patient with me from time to time and have served over the years as sounding boards for the concepts presented in this book.

Ben G. Baldwin

THE COMPLETE BOOK OF INSURANCE

ONE

INTRODUCTION

Surveys have shown that professional advisers, attorneys, CPAs and financial planners feel ill-equipped to advise you on personal risk management matters. These professionals have the same trouble you do in deciding *when* to insure, *what* to insure and *how much* to pay for insurance benefits. How then can you make these decisions without spending an inordinate amount of money and time?

Consider how much of your income goes to pay for insurance. You pay for social security. If you are employed, your employer pays an amount equal to what you pay into your social security account. Additionally, your employer is paying between 25 percent and 40 percent of your gross annual earnings into various employee benefit plans designed to protect your economic security. You pay for homeowner's policies, condominium policies and renters policies. You pay for insurance on the vehicle you drive. Since you might inadvertently cause harm to another individual, you pay for liability insurances. You pay for disability insurance in case sickness or accident one day prevents you from earning a living. You also pay for health insurance to protect you against medical catastrophe.

Your employer or the government assists you in paying for some of these coverages, but bear in mind that if your employer helps, it is as part of your compensation package and a result of your personal efforts for that employer. Therefore, it is being paid for out of *your* earnings. The government's assistance is being paid for with your tax dollars. The government has no other way to come up with money. Your fellow taxpayers may be also helping but don't ever think that the money isn't coming out of your pocket also.

Clearly, insurance expenses represent a large portion of your budget This book is designed to help you spend that money wisely, and to make the process of buying insurance as easy and convenient as possible. Each chapter will help you identify and understand your current exposure to risk, and will help you analyze those exposures and decide how the risks that you must live with should be managed. The book makes it easy for you to compare the insurance coverage that you need to the insurance coverage you presently have. You will be able to implement a personal risk management program in which you buy insurance when you should, don't buy insurance when you shouldn't, and have cost-effective benefits in force when you need them.

This book is not designed to circumvent the insurance professionals who earn commissions selling insurance products, it is designed to make sure they earn those commissions by giving you valuable assistance and quality products. It is designed to help you select competent insurance advisors and to use them well in helping you to save time and money.

Two primary tools within this book will assist you in your personal risk management program. The first is the inventory page. The inventory page will help you gather the important information from your existing insurances so you can evaluate the benefits you presently have and what they are costing you. The second tool is the "Action Letter." The "Action Letters" are rough drafts of letters from you to your insurance providers specifying what you want and what you need to know in order to make your insurance decisions. They will help acquire from insurance professionals, the information on benefits and costs that will allow you to insure wisely.

Sometimes it is difficult to tell the difference between the insurance professional and the insurance peddler—an important distinction. The insurance professional seeks to understand you, your problems and opportunities, and to direct your purchases toward products that will enhance your own and your family's security at acceptable and appropriate costs. The insurance peddler, on the other hand, is merely interested in making a sale and not concerned with whether or not the product fits your situation. Making the distinction is not easy. All insurance salespeople become suspect and people are reluctant to accept good advice from knowledgeable and caring professionals. This book will help you distinguish the peddler from the pro, and the good advice from the sales talk.

To Insure? . . . or Not To Insure?

Personal risk management means dealing with uncertainty in your life. This uncertainty exists because you are constantly exposed to the possibility of loss, injury, disadvantage or destruction. The risks we are dealing with do not have the potential to make you rich: in this book, to win the battle of living in an uncertain world is to experience no *loss*. We cannot assure you that you will experience no loss if insurance is the only tool you use to assist you in dealing with risk.

Take a look at the risk management illustration in Figure 1–1. That diagram begins with the risk identification phase of your personal risk management program. We are all concerned with the risks to which we are personally exposed and the risks to which our family members are exposed for which we are responsible. What you do to earn a living and what you do for fun and recreation determines many of the risks to which you are exposed daily. Your family relationships and responsibilities produce additional risks. What you own and what you owe, your sources of support, and your spending habits all reveal additional risks. You will find as you com-

Figure 1–1
Risk Management Illustration

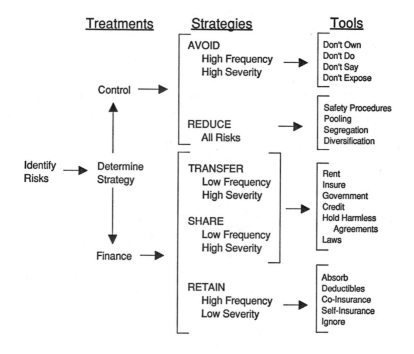

plete the policy inventory forms in the following chapters that, although you may have identified and managed many risks, you may have overlooked others that are not adequately provided for under your existing policies. Your concern for others, be they family members or not, may also expose you to personal economic loss because you are, in effect, an important part of their economic security. If a risk in their lives would jeopardize your economic security, it's an area of potential loss that requires management.

Risk Treatment

As you identify each risk, you will have to determine how to treat it. You basically have two choices. You can seek to control the uncertainty to which you are exposed, or to finance it. We will first discuss control.

Your mother's advice on how to handle risk (and you still hear it today, no matter what your age) was "Be careful." Her method of handling risks was to reduce them by practicing caution. She was encouraging safety procedures which we all observe to one degree or another.

However, the reduction and caution strategy does not compensate adequately for certain risks. Some risks are of such high severity and, under certain circumstances, of such high frequency that the best strategy is to avoid them entirely. For example, if you own a three-wheel, all-terrain vehicle that your thirteen-year-old drives recklessly at high speed over unfamiliar territory, the consequences of that action are so severe and will happen with such high frequency, that the primary recommendation to you would be to get rid of the vehicle. Should you reject that advice, the next suggestion would be to institute Mother's method of handling this exposure to risk— control. You could fix the all-terrain vehicle so it couldn't go too fast, make sure the vehicle is only driven over familiar territory and make sure that proper safety equipment is used at all times the vehicle is being operated. Trading it in on the four-wheeled variety would be another alternative to control your exposure to risk.

To handle these high severity, high frequency risks, remember the "don'ts." *Don't* own it, *don't* do it, *don't* say it, *don't* expose yourself to that particular risk. Once control strategies have been implemented to the maximum degree possible, risks that can be avoided have been avoided, and risks that cannot be avoided have been reduced to the greatest extent possible. The next strategies dealing with risk are financing strategies. We need others to assist us in financing risks that happen infrequently and are so severe that they threaten our economic security.

In most cases, when we seek to finance our exposure to risk with the assistance of insurance companies, we find that most companies will accept the obligation to "share" our exposure to risk rather than accepting 100% of the responsibility for the loss if it should occur. The reason for this is that if we have arranged for the financing of a risk by paying a small amount (accepting a small personal loss in the way of a premium payment), so that an insurance company or governmental agency will pick up 100% of the loss if some contingency would occur, we become less careful than we should be. A good example of this is the Federal Deposit Insurance for banks and Savings and Loans. As a result of the fact that depositors theoretically could not lose, they did not concern themselves with the economic strength of the organization to which they sent their deposits. They merely concerned themselves with the amount of interest they would earn. The managers of those organizations could pay higher interest to those depositors if they made high interest rate loans to less creditworthy borrowers and since managers also were in a situation where they felt they could not lose, nothing held them back. Nobody was being careful; the results are inevitable. Now taxpayers, will have to pay for cleaning up the Savings and Loan mess.

Sharing risks, on the other hand, seems to make everyone involved more careful. You will find insurance companies, the government and the government agencies much more willing to pick up the major economic loss of risks that you and I are exposed to if we will share with them in those losses via deductibles and co-insurances, e.g., they will pay 80% of the loss if we will pay 20%.

There are certain risks that we just have to live with. They happen with such high frequency and/or cause losses of such low severity that they cannot be shared economically with others. You can provide financing for them through your personal budget and manage them by being as careful as possible. Many people have difficulty recognizing these risks and they try to insure them. As a result they pay exorbitant premiums for unneeded insurances that have little prospect of paying meaningful benefits. They have, in effect, taken a potential opportunity for loss and turned it into a certain loss by paying an exorbitant premium to the insurance company.

This book, then, is just as much about when *not* to insure as it is about when and how to insure. In the following chapters we will identify your risk exposure to determine how to treat that risk, whether to control it or to finance it. When you have learned to evaluate your opportunities to avoid risk, reduce risk, transfer risk, share risk or retain risk, you can implement the appropriate strategies for managing risk.

What Is Insurance?

"A device for the elimination or reduction of an economic risk, to all members of a large group by employing a system of equitable contributions out of which losses are paid."

Webster's Third International Dictionary

"A plan by which large numbers of people associate themselves and transfer risks that attach to individuals to the shoulders of all."

General Insurance, David L. Bizkelhaupt, 1979, page 28

These two definitions reveal two fundamental characteristics of insurance. First, it is a method of shifting risk from you, one individual, to a group. As people join this group in ever increasing numbers in order to avoid a particular type of risk to which all are exposed, the risk for the group becomes more and more certain. To you, the loss *might* occur whereas to the total group, the loss *will* occur, at some particular statistical rate. The accuracy with which this particular rate of occurrence can be predicted determines how much each member of the group must pay in order to provide funds to cover the losses experienced by that small statistical portion of the total group. The second fundamental characteristic then, is that insurance is an arrangement for paying for inevitable losses and is thus a risk financing method.

There are any number of groups that you may join in order to pool your potential risks so that, should you be the statistic, the group will assist you in keeping to a minimum the economic loss to which you are exposed. There may be a "pass the hat" type of benefit, so that if some unfortunate occurrence should befall a member, the other members come to that person's aid.

As a result of being a citizen of the United States and paying your income and social security taxes, you are involved in social insurance that is required by law and administered by the government. These programs are concerned with the social adequacy of the benefits provided and are usually designed to provide for at least minimum economic security. Examples of these social insurances are: social security, medicare, state workers compensation laws, unemployment compensation, some state sponsored disability and compulsory automobile insurance programs, the railroad retirement and unemployment and disability systems, and so on. The benefits and costs of these various programs are determined by the laws that brought them into existence.

There are certain governmental or society programs for which you do not pay directly but which are paid for out of your federal and/or state income taxes, such as old age assistance, aid to the blind, aid to dependent children and medicaid. Society—that is, you, the taxpayer—pays for these programs, not the recipients.

The government also provides various public insurance programs which, although not mandatory, have been established to benefit the entire community. Those who wish to avail themselves of the benefits join these public insurance programs by voluntarily paying the costs. The government makes available to you FHA mortgage insurance, crop insurance, government military life insurance programs, Federal Deposit insurance, flood insurance, securities investors protection insurance, pension benefit guaranteed insurance, supplemental insurance for the aged and, in some cases, riot insurance and even surety bonds for minority contractors.

Insurance: Economic Lubricant

Through such programs, society is fulfilling its obligation to provide a basic economic lubricant, insurance, where the private insurance companies have been unable to provide it.

It can easily be imagined that under certain circumstances the presence of risk could paralyze you into inaction. If the only way to avoid risk was not to do, not to say, not to own and basically not to expose yourself to risk, you would be extremely limited in what you could do. Would a lender lend you a substantial amount of money for a mortgage on your house if there wasn't fire insurance? Can you envision a society without medical insurance? Would you take the chance of driving a vehicle without insurance?

The functions of insurance are to provide you with peace of mind, assistance in economic survival, a basis for credit, indemnification in case of loss, solutions to social problems and a means of increasing your ability to use your assets. It also serves society by stimulating savings and providing investment capital.

TWO

DISABILITY INSURANCE

Disability

"The inability to pursue an occupation or perform services for wages because of physical or mental impairment."

"A physical or mental illness, injury, or condition that incapacitates in any way."

Webster's Third New International Dictionary

Some readers may feel that disability income insurance is not a consideration for them since they need not work for wages. They may be retired or able to live on investment income. If the first definition of disability above—"The inability to pursue an occupation or perform services FOR WAGES because of physical or mental impairment"—was the only definition of disability, they might be right. However, we will also deal with what we refer to as "functional disability,"

13

which is better described by the second of the above definitions—"A physical or mental illness, injury, or condition that
incapacitates in any way."

To be unable to work for wages brings earning ability
down to zero; to be functionally disabled brings earnings
below zero. We become an economic burden to others who
must provide for our needs. We will deal with functional disability, and the associated nursing home and long-term care
coverages, in this chapter.

The reason we address disability so early in this book is
because so few readers have adequate coverage. Statistically
speaking, less than one in six people reading this book own
enough disability income insurance protection to provide for a
disability lasting for more than two years. If you experience a
disability that lasts for more than 90 days, you can expect the
average duration of that disability to be at least five years. A
disability, will not only terminate your income, but will
probably increase your costs for medicines, medical care and
associated care expenses. This is commonly referred to as the
"double whammy" of disability—no income and high medical
bills. Disability in its most difficult form is referred to as the
"living death." For some of the functionally disabled, and
those who care for them, the concept that there is something
worse than death is very real. This coverage is so important
that it deserves to be the first coverage we consider.

Many people own life insurance and are concerned with
the risk of dying, but look at the statistics in Figure 2–1. The
risk of a disability lasting 90 days or more exceeds the risk of
death by three and one-half times for a 32-year old, and three
times for a 42-year old and almost twice for a 62-year old.

If you have trouble visualizing yourself disabled, con-
gratulations. Be happy you are so healthy now. But as you
look around you, notice the beveled curbs in the sidewalks.
Who are they for? What about the larger stall in the rest
rooms and the reserved parking spaces? The people using
them were probably just like you at one time.

If you do not need disability insurance, either you are
able to live on income-producing investments that others
manage for you, or you can't visualize yourself disabled and

Figure 2–1
Disability/Death Odds

Age	Chances of a 90 Day or More Disability vs. Death
22	3.6 to 1
32	3.5 to 1
42	3.0 to 1
52	2.3 to 1
62	1.8 to 1

Source: 1964 Commissioners Disability Table
1958 C.S.O Mortality Table

the economic results of that disability. What would happen if you took a six-month vacation, or a year off without pay? If it would have no economic effect on you or your family why don't you do it? If it would...you need disability income insurance. The next question is where to obtain it?

Government Disability Plans

Although it is true that social security will provide benefits for disabled workers, it has been reported that 75% of all individual disability claims to social security are being denied. Social Security is using a definition of disability based on what are referred to as daily work activities or the social security anachronism, DWAs. The DWAs are "standing, walking, sitting, lifting, pushing, pulling, reaching, carrying, understanding and carrying out and remembering simple instructions." Your ability to do any of these daily work activities can result in your claim for disability benefits being declined. Social security defines disability " . . . as an inability to engage in any substantial gainful activity by reason of any medically determinable physical or mental impairment that can be expected to result in death or which has lasted or can be expected to last for a continuous period of not less than 12 months." The 75% declination of claims rate combined with the tough definition of disability and the fact that the Social Security Administration is going through severe personnel cutbacks and budget restraints all indicate that you should not depend upon social security to provide for your disability income needs.

What about state mandated worker's compensation laws that impose absolute liability on an employer for certain injuries suffered by employees in the course of their work? Won't that provide for you? Not if you are *not* disabled on the job! Also, consider the adequacy of amount and duration of worker's compensation payments. Most of you will find that the benefits provided by your state are inadequate in amount and are payable for too short a time to provide for your real needs.

If you live in California, Hawaii, New Jersey, New York, Rhode Island or Puerto Rico, you probably have access to a state sponsored compulsory temporary disability plan that is designed to provide income to disabled workers from "non-occupational" causes. These programs provide a base of benefits upon which you can build; however, they are insufficient as a total provider for your personal disability income needs.

Association Disability Insurance

You may be a member of an organization or association that offers group disability income benefits to its membership. Some of these plans are very enticing because of their low cost, but beware! These plans are sometimes inadequate because they have weak definitions of disability. You would not be considered disabled even if the only thing you could possibly do would be to sell pencils on the street corner. In addition, many offer benefits only in the event of accident and/or only for a very limited period of time. Also, you personally do not control what happens to such a plan. It may be cancelled! If the insurance provider for your organization decides to terminate the offer of this plan, you may find yourself trying to replace the benefits at what could be a very inopportune time. You may actually be disabled or in ill health—a situation in which no one else will insure you, so that you cannot replace the benefits. For the moment, imagine yourself as an attorney in the State of Illinois insured within your Bar Association plan. In 1989 the membership received a communication that stated in part that the association sponsored insurance programs had been terminated or would be terminating throughout the year. Some of the members who availed themselves of these plans may already be disabled or too sick to replace this coverage, and although they have enjoyed the relatively low rates the plan offered while they were insured, they may now be in a very difficult situation. Similar insurance company problems have occurred in the American Medical Association plans in the past. Do not depend upon association group insurance for your primary disability insurance needs.

Employer-Provided Disability Insurance

Employers also often offer group disability income insurance plans. Just as in the association plans, it will be important for you to check the benefits provided by the plan both for duration and quality.

The advantage of employer-provided group disability income insurance is its low cost. With employer-provided plans, you do have the employer as an advocate to deal with the insurance company. He is interested in making sure that you have sufficient coverage and that it is the highest quality coverage obtainable. However, neither you nor your employer controls the insurance company's choice whether to continue to offer the coverage or not. If the insurance company finds that providing benefits for your employer has become economically unfeasible, that insurance carrier may well decide to cancel that coverage. This lack of personal control is the primary disadvantage of employer-provided group disability income insurance. Additionally, there may be restrictions regarding the amounts and durations of benefits, the definition of disability, the integration of the benefits provided by the plan with those provided by social security and/or any other sources of disability income benefits, and the probable lack of your ability to continue the coverage should you terminate employment with that employer.

The bottom line is that these government, association and employer-sponsored coverages do not give *you* sufficient control over your benefits. You lack the ability to maintain these benefits in force for the entire period you deem them necessary, the ability to know exactly what they will cost and the assurance that they will pay when your income is decreased or stopped due to disability.

Consider this situation. If there was a medical insurance product that you could buy today that contained a guarantee that the contract could not be cancelled and that the cost to you could not be raised, you probably would buy it happily and quickly. The guarantee of health insurance at a guaranteed price would be a wonderful benefit. Such a medical insurance product is not available. No one could issue a policy like this in light of today's uncontrolled increases in medical care costs.

But such a disability income policy *is available* for purchase by *individuals* today. This type of policy should be the cornerstone for your disability income insurance.

Individually Owned Disability Insurance

The most desirable disability income insurance is an individually owned (not group) disability income policy issued by an insurance company that states that the contract may not be cancelled during your entire working life, and that furthermore stipulates that the insurance company may never, during that period of time, charge you any more than is specified in the policy on the date the policy is issued. This is referred to as non-cancellable and guaranteed renewable coverage.

The policy should be the highest quality policy available. It should define disability as your being unable to perform as required within your own occupation. That definition of disability should insure you within your own occupation for as long as possible, preferably for life.

This non-cancellable, guaranteed renewable long-term disability insurance is at a peak in its development in 1988. It was a buyer's market in which good companies were aggressively seeking business and price competition was high—but the market is changing. It is to your advantage to get today's prices locked in for a lifetime. Prices are expected to increase in the future because claims have been going up faster than expected. The risk of disability is increasing substantially today because the killer diseases no longer kill quickly . . . they disable. AIDS-related claims are up, and disability claims by women are higher than the insurance industry had anticipated. All of this will increase prices and restrict supply. No one knows the importance of disability insurance as well as one who cannot buy it at any price.

How Much Disability Insurance Should You Have?

Let's get to the details of the policy we have just described above. We could get very scientific about this by dissecting your budget to determine what expenses would terminate, what expenses would remain and what expenses would increase if you were disabled. We could use a great deal of care in estimating the amount of such expenses in order to determine as accurately as possible the amount of disability income insurance you should have. Or we could say to the insurance company, "Make me an offer. How much disability income insurance will you issue to me?" That's a frightening prospect, because it obviously is in the interests of the insurance company to issue you as much insurance as they can, and to sell as much of their product as they can. Also, the agent wants to sell you the largest policy possible, since his commission will increase with an increased premium. What's to keep this situation under control?

Actually, the insurance company tries very hard not to 'over-insure' you for disability. As you recall, we have asked the insurance company to pay these benefits for as long as possible—preferably for the rest of your life—if you should be disabled that long. What would encourage you to go back to work? Insurance companies feel that you will be encouraged to go back to work, thus relieving them of their obligation of continuing to pay benefits, if you have some economic incentive, i.e., if you can make more money by going back to work than you can by continuing to receive the benefits of your disability income policy. Obviously, the insurance company will offer you something less than 100% of your regular earnings. How much less?

It depends upon who is paying for the policy. Income taxes make the difference. Uncle Sam encourages *you* to buy and pay for your own disability income insurance through a tax law which states that if you have purchased and paid for your own disability income insurance policies, then the benefits paid to you as result of a disability are to be delivered without the imposition of current income taxes. Suppose your policy states that in the event of your disability, your benefits will be $1,000 per month. If you have paid for that policy with your after-tax earnings, that $1,000 is delivered month after month without any taxation whatsoever. However, if you have paid that premium with pre-tax dollars through some employer plan or if your employer had paid those premiums for you and not added the cost of those benefits to your W-2 compensation, then those benefits would be subject to ordinary income taxation. It is highly likely that 28% or more, depending upon your marginal state and federal income tax bracket, would have to go to Uncle Sam. To be disabled and pay almost a third of your benefits to the government is not a good arrangement. Too frequently we find employers paying for their employees' disability income group insurance benefits. This shows a lack of understanding in the design of benefit plans. We suggest you ask your employer to allow you to pay for those benefits with your after-tax dollars, i.e., pay taxes on the cost of the plan. You will find the very small amount of tax payable on the relatively low cost of group disability benefits during your healthy working years is much easier to handle than the reduction in income due to taxation during a disability.

Employers can also help you buy individually owned non-cancellable, guaranteed renewable disability income insurance policies (the kind recommended) that are entirely portable. In spite of the fact that, in most cases, you personally would be paying the entire premium on that policy, it still would be less expensive than if you were to buy the identical policy on your own. Insurance companies frequently will discount rates up to 10-15% for policies that they can bill to one billing address. In some cases, they will even make it a little easier for you to qualify for such policies. Since each participant would be paying the premium for such policies with after-tax dollars, there are no participation requirements or discrimination problems with such plans. If you want help with disability income insurance, ask your employer if he would allow such policies to be purchased by way of salary deduction by you and your fellow employees who elect to purchase them.

The insurance company will limit the amount of disability income it will issue to you to approximately 60-70% of your compensation up to $100,000 per year when you are paying for the policy with your own after-tax income. That way, they know that if you are disabled and collecting 60-70% of your regular compensation without having to pay taxes on it, it is equivalent in spending power to almost 100% of your after-tax earnings. For those earning over $100,000 per year the percentage of income the insurance company will offer will be less than 60%. It is perfectly appropriate for you to ask an insurance company how much they will issue you. If you accept all that the insurance company will allow you to buy, you have done your best to provide for your own and your family's security. It is highly unlikely that you would consider the benefit payment too large in the event that you did become disabled.

Accident and/or Sickness Benefits

Some policies stipulate that benefits will be payable for life if the insured is disabled as a result of accident, yet pay benefits for only two years if disability is caused by sickness. Such policies are inadequate and should not be accepted unless nothing better may be obtained. Your policy should stipulate that benefits will be payable for as long as possible, regardless of what has caused your disability, illness or accident.

How Long Should Benefits Be Payable?

You may not be able to obtain a policy that will guarantee to pay disability benefits for the rest of your life in the event of your disability. Insurance companies require many qualifications in order to issue such contracts. Nevertheless, that is what I suggest that you ask for. If the insurance company is unable to issue a policy that provides benefit payments for life, they will then offer you the next closest thing to it. Your question to the insurance company is, Why? If another company will issue lifetime benefits, then maybe, all other things being equal, you should deal with the company that offers you the longest benefit period.

The bottom line specification for how long benefits should be payable is: for as long as you can get them payable. You don't want benefits that will terminate in the middle of a disability!

How Soon Should Benefits Begin?

Insurance companies can issue policies that will begin your disability benefits the moment you are disabled, but they can be very expensive. If you want to reduce the cost of your policy, you could allow the insurance company to defer benefit payments until a period of time after your disability occurs. If you can wait 30, 60 or 90 days; referred to as an "elimination" or a "waiting period," you will find a substantial reduction in premium. You would be wise to accept the 90-day waiting period if you have sufficient resources because often this is the most cost-effective choice. Remember that the insurance company pays the benefit at the end of the month in which it is due, so with a 90-day waiting period, you would receive your first benefit payment 120 days after the start of the disability.

Get exact pricing information from the insurance agent who will be providing the coverage for you, who will earn a commission as a result of designing and providing the plan that meets your specifications.

Definition of Disability

Disability may be defined as the inability of the insured, due to injury or sickness, to engage in the substantial and material duties of *his or her regular occupation*. Alternatively, disability may be defined as the inability of the insured to engage in *Any Occupation*. A compromise definition of disability between these two would be the inability of the insured to engage in any occupation for which he or she is *Reasonably qualified by reason of training, education and experience*.

Your disability income insurance policy should specify that you are disabled if, as a result of an injury or sickness, you are unable to engage in the substantial and material duties of your *own* occupation, your regular occupation. This is referred to as "OWN OCC." In most circumstances, however, it is not possible to have that definition stay in force for the rest of your life. You will frequently find policies offering an "OWN CCC" definition for a limited period followed by a "reasonable CCC" definition. This is referred to as a "split definition." As we have recommended with the previous specifications, ask first. Tell the insurance company what you want and find out the best that they will offer, then determine if that is good enough or not. If it is not good enough, seek alternative offers from other insurance companies and accept the best offer you find.

The Can Do, Can't Do Period

Following a period of disability, there is frequently a time during which you can do some things and cannot do others; partial disability, so to speak. You would prefer not to have the benefits of your disability income policy stop immediately as you go through a period of trying to go back to work on less than a full-time basis. Insurance companies have two phrases to define this set of circumstances; *partial disability and residual disability.*

Partial disability relates to what you are able to do. You suffer partial disability if you can do only part of the material and substantial duties of your occupation. Therefore, to the extent that you are partially disabled, at least part of your benefits should be payable.

Residual disability on the other hand, relates to your earning power. You suffer partial disability if you are not able to earn what you used to earn. It provides benefits proportionate to the loss of your earning power, regardless of the type of work you do and how you are compensated. A commissioned salesperson, a self-employed person or someone who has built his own business may find himself one day able to do only part of his work; however, he may be able to earn as much as he did before he was disabled which could result in no benefits being paid under the residual rider. If the policy he purchased had a residual disability benefit within it which related the payment of benefits under the policy to his earnings, the insurance company would, in order to determine if his earning power had been effected, request copies of his income tax forms and business tax forms in order to verify earnings. Many people would find this unpleasant, and would prefer to have benefits based upon their ability "to do" rather than their ability "to earn."

Such partial disability or residual disability provisions may not be part of your basic policy, but may be purchased as riders. It is the basic contract that is of primary importance. Do not let the continuing debate regarding partial or residual riders paralyze you into inaction—get a policy in force.

Policy Provisions

Examine your current policy or the one you are considering putting in force for the following policy provisions.

Renewability of Your Policy. Look for the policy to be non-cancellable and guaranteed renewable to age 65. Make sure the premiums cannot be increased beyond what is stated in the contract. This provision makes this personal policy the keystone of your disability security plans.

Duration of Benefits. After the cost-effective elimination period you have chosen, the policy should pay a monthly income while you are totally disabled because of accident or sickness for the maximum benefit period you can obtain.

Definition of Disability. You want total disability defined as your inability to perform the material and substantial duties of "your regular occupation" ("own OCC"), in any period of continuous disability for as long as possible.

Waiver of Premium. After total disability has lasted for 90 days, the insurance company should waive any premium that becomes due while disability lasts.

Recurrence of Disability. If the same disability recurs within six months after you go back to work, it should not be considered a new disability, you should not have to satisfy another waiting period, and benefits should be payable immediately.

Free Look. State laws mandate that you have ten days to review your new policy. If you decide you don't want to keep it, send it back to the agent or company within ten days and request that it be annulled. The company will then refund all premiums you have paid. Submit your request in writing and get a written acknowledgment that it has been received for cancellation.

Grace Period. State laws also require a 31-day grace period. This means that if a premium after the first one is not paid by the due date, it may be paid during the 31 days that follow. During the grace period the policy should stay in force.

Policy Options

The following are some of the options that may be available on your disability income policy and a basic description of how each works. There are substantial differences among companies offering these options. Your licensed disability professional can be helpful to you in choosing what is best for you.

CPI Cost-of-Living Adjustments. After a year of continuous disability, the amount of total and residual benefits will increase in some proportion to the increase in the annual Consumer Price Index (CPI) each year you continue to be disabled. This option is available only on long-term plans and is sometimes referred to as an inflation rider. Watch for significant differences among companies offering this rider. Check if the increases are calculated on a simple interest basis or compounded—it makes a big difference! Also check for limits on how high the increases can go.

Residual Disability Income. If you return to work while residually disabled, you will receive a monthly benefit in proportion to your percentage loss of income.

Guaranteed Insurability. This allows you to purchase additional monthly income periodically subject to the insurance company's issue and financial underwriting requirements but without evidence of medical insurability. This is strongly recommended.

Social Security Supplement. During the first year of disability this option will allow you to receive a monthly benefit of a stipulated sum in addition to the basic monthly income. After the first year, the benefit will be paid in any month for which Social Security disability benefits are not payable. It may be payable to age 65. It is available only on long-term plans.

Hospital Confinement. The monthly income and any Supplemental Income or Social Security Supplement may be paid for any part of the elimination period during which you are confined in a hospital as a result of total disability.

Family Income. You may receive a stipulated amount of additional monthly income from the end of the elimination period to the end of a stipulated period of time which begins on the date of issue. This rider can be used for specific limited term financial obligations such as a mortgage or college costs.

Some of these options may be more important to you than others. A good cost-of-living adjustment rider, which is strongly recommended, will provide an effective inflation fighting plan for disability protection by providing automatic increases to your benefits after one year of disability. Some of these riders will provide an increase in benefits automatically, regardless of what has happened to the CPI. Others will be keyed to actual changes in the CPI. In any case, the rider should be designed to make sure your disability income goes up as prices go up in the future.

I also am in favor of the guaranteed insurability rider. This rider allows you to purchase additional monthly disability income insurance up to a stipulated amount as long as your income qualifies for such increases, regardless of your current health status. Since disability income insurance is very carefully underwritten by insurance companies, health is a very important question. Think about what health conditions might prevent you from earning a living. How about a bad back, migraine headaches, the loss of a finger, a bad accident on the ski slopes, problems with your balance, something that interferes with your thinking or speaking? Any number of things can seriously impair your ability to work, and once any of these has occurred, it will be very difficult for you to get disability income insurance. The guaranteed insurability rider solves this problem!

Return of Premium Rider

This option appeals to those who can't conceive of themselves as disabled—the "I'm as healthy as a horse" group. Since they never expect to make a claim on their policy, they like the feature that promises to return a portion of their premium, less claims paid, at some future dates, such as every five years. These riders are not cheap. For example, you have a return of premium rider that guarantees you a 60% return of premiums paid if you have no claims for five years. Your annual premium is $2,777, so you would have paid in $13,885 over the five years and would be expecting 60% of that ($8,331) to be returned to you if you had no claims. The cost of the return of premium rider is $1,190 per year.

The way to evaluate the offer is to use your calculator to compound the value of the $1,190 payment for the five years which you must pay to get back the $8,331. Enter the following:

$1,190 (payment) (beginning)
Time = 5 years
Future value = $8,331
Solve for interest rate = 11.438%

The conclusion is that if you were to put the $1,190 elsewhere you would have to earn 11.4% to match the benefit payable from the policy. The problem is that the $8,331 due you from the policy is payable only *if* the policy is still in force and only *if* you have not reduced it by making a claim. These "if" statements create risk that the payment will not be made. It also may influence you not to make a legitimate claim when you deserve to be paid. This could mean that the cost of the return of premium rider came out of your own pocket because, in order to get your refund, you passed up claiming benefits that should have been paid to you due to disability.

In most cases we suggest investing the extra premium required for this rider into a mutual fund within your life insurance policy or an annuity contract (no current taxes on earnings) so as to avoid the risk of total loss. I will continue to recommend declining the rider until such time as the insurance companies design it so that the consumer is not exposed to such a great risk of loss and can expect a reasonable return on the extra funds paid for the rider.

Other Kinds of Disability Income Insurance

In addition to the high quality disability income policies that replace income in the event of disability, there also are policies that will pay the overhead expense for sole proprietors and/or professional service providers during periods of disability. There are disability policies designed to serve various business needs. What would happen if your business partner were disabled and unable to carry his share of the load in operating the business? If it became necessary for you to buy out that disabled partner's interest in the business, where would you get the money, particularly now that you are running the business by yourself? The answer may be in a disability buy-out policy that is designed for just this type of business circumstance.

The Inventory

Complete the following inventory of all disability income policies you currently have in force. Record who is insured, the insuring company, policy number, the monthly income, when benefits start, how long they last, and the cost. Circle the numbers that indicate the important features of your policy.

Now that you have completed the inventory of your existing disability income insurance policies, it is time to review them in light of the previous discussion. If you have circled 1, 2 and 3, it would appear that you have purchased quality disability income insurance. Number 1 indicates a personal policy; number 2, a non-cancellable guaranteed renewable contract; and number 3, that it insures you within your own occupation. If your policy includes features 4, 5, or 6, see if it can be replaced or supplemented by a policy featuring 1, 2, and 3. If you also have circled 7 or 8, 9, and 10, indicating that your policy has either a partial or residual disability rider, a guaranteed insurability rider and an inflation rider, you have selected some of the most important riders currently available within disability income policies. Keep in mind that the quality of your policy is extremely dependent upon the quality of the insurance company that underwrites it. You expect that insurance company to deal with you fairly in the event of disability. Inevitably, in some circumstances it will be difficult to determine if one is truly disabled. Individually, of course, you prefer to have the insurance company always err in your favor. However, it is also the obligation of your insurance company to stay in business so that in the future it can serve you, personally in the event of disability. When you own a disability income policy with a particular company, it is in your best interest that they not pay unwarranted claims.

Take Action

In order to put a disability income policy in force, you will need to contact an agent licensed to sell disability income

Figure 2-2
The Inventory

Company/ Insured	Policy Number	Monthly Income	Benefits Start	Benefits End	Annual Premium	Features of Disability (circle as many as apply)
						1 2 3 4 5 6 7 8 9 10
						1 2 3 4 5 6 7 8 9 10
						1 2 3 4 5 6 7 8 9 10
						1 2 3 4 5 6 7 8 9 10
						1 2 3 4 5 6 7 8 9 10

Total: Total:

70% of my gross monthly income is $ _____ .

Features of Disability

1 Personal Policy

2. Non-Cancellable & Guaranteed Renewable

3. Your Own Occupation

4. Group Policy

5. Association Policy

6 Any Occupation

7. Partial Disability

8. Residual Disability

9. Guaranteed Insurability

10. Inflation Rider

policies in your state. A professional salesperson should be able to help you find quality coverage from a quality company. The following Action Letter should be of value to you in dealing with these professional salespeople.

A professional salesperson will help you find out what is currently available in this field. It takes a full-time participant in the marketplace to offer you the most assistance. The disability income marketplace is constantly changing, and it has been improving for the consumer. There are much better contracts available today at more competitive costs than were generally available even five years ago, but act now—it won't last long! It is important for you to know that recently the costs for this type of coverage have been increasing, rather than decreasing as they had been doing up to 1989. Drug and alcohol abuse is resulting in more mental health and stress claims. There also are more pregnancy claims from today's baby boomers. Arthritis, back, knee and foot problems also occur more frequently as a result of overambitious joggers. Recently it has been reported that companies have increased men's rates 6-10% and women's rates as much as 35%. The majority of companies charging the same rates for men and women have experienced more moderate increases. Those who lock in today's rates with a quality contract will be extremely happy that they had the foresight to do so.

The Action Letter was designed to allow you to specify your needs for a disability income policy to a professional agent. The first paragraph of the letter presents your request. The second paragraph states your objectives as we have suggested them to you. The third paragraph specifies a policy with a specific monthly income so that you will be able to compare the quotes that you receive from a number of different insurance companies. This paragraph also suggests that you want the agent's help in evaluating various supplemental benefits or riders that are available with a disability income policy. Many of you will be pleasantly surprised at the personal concern that the true professional will show in encouraging you to purchase those riders which are of value and discouraging you from buying those riders which may not be cost effective.

Figure 2–3
Action Letter

Dear_____:

I am a full time _____ and I am in the process of evaluating my disability income insurance and would appreciate your assistance.

In the event of my disability, it is my objective to have disability income benefits of approximately sixty to seventy percent of my income, with the strongest definition of disability available. Preferably, the policy should insure me within my occupational specialty for the duration of the benefit period.

I would appreciate a quote for quality individual, non-cancellable, guaranteed renewable coverage in the amount of $_____ per month for the longest payment period possible, preferably for life. Please quote a 30, 60, 90, 180, and 365 day waiting period, and with both a step rate and level premium plan if both are available. Your quote should include any supplemental benefits that you would recommend for me along with descriptive material and premiums.

Please mail proposals to me from one/two/three/four quality companies. I would appreciate your recommendations regarding which suit my needs best.

Please call me at _____ if you have questions.

Sincerely,

Feel free to ask the agent to show you his or her personal policy. Discuss the riders he accepted and those he did not accept, and why. The agent's response will be a measure of his quality. If that agent doesn't respond in a helpful, positive manner don't buy from him! You have an obligation to yourself to hire and pay only people who are well qualified to serve you and who earn their fee.

For some unknown reason many people buy from the first agent who knocks on their door. They not only cheat themselves, but do a disservice to the insurance industry as well. This type of consumer contributes to the continued success of unqualified and unscrupulous agents whose only positive quality is their ability to knock on doors and keep on knocking. I encourage you to be pro-active. Seek out a highly qualified professional. Help the industry get rid of the unscrupulous and unqualified—don't hire them.

The fourth paragraph of the Action Letter asks the insurance professional to obtain proposals for you from a number of different quality insurance companies. This paragraph is designed to do two things for you. First, it is designed to obtain competitive cost information from "quality" companies. Second, by asking the professional to recommend the proposal that will best suit your needs, you find out if this person's advice and counsel is worth the commissions you'll be charged. In short, you should hire an insurance professional as you would any other counsel, based on what he can do for you that you cannot do as well for yourself. There are two very important qualifications that you should always look for in a salesperson that are more important than all the professional designations in the world: a personal concern for your welfare and personal integrity. It is incumbent upon you to seek out and determine if your representative has these two qualifications. You are not likely to be very satisfied with purchases made from an individual who lacks them.

Long-Term Care Insurance

Americans spent $35.2 billion on nursing home care in 1985. The sources of funds for these payments are in Figure 2–4.

Figure 2–4 indicates that the high costs for long-term care are being paid by you! You pay almost 95% of these bills either individually, with your family's help or as a taxpayer. Statistics indicate that upon entering a nursing facility, the typical patient is paying the bill from personal or family savings—that's the 51.4%. When the personal and family savings have been exhausted and the patient has been "spent down" to Medicaid, the person is considered destitute by his or her state of residence and qualifies for welfare benefits from Medicaid. Now, you, the taxpayer, must pay the bill. It has been reported that it normally takes approximately 22 months before the average nursing home resident's resources are entirely exhausted. It is obvious that families and individuals typically are not prepared to meet this need. State politicians tell us that welfare medicaid funds are insufficient to meet the demands that are being put upon them. Medicare is not the answer since it is only paying 1.7% of the bill. So, unless you have some of those "other sources," it looks like private insurance is the most economical and appropriate method to meet this need.

The group over age 65 is the fastest growing segment of our population. Statistically speaking, two thirds of the people who have ever reached age 65 from the beginning of time are alive today. This group looks forward to twenty good, productive years after retirement. Someday they can expect to reach a point of diminishing capabilities. They will be the most substantial consumers of health services. Just as we all needed care when we came into this world, it is likely that we will need care as we leave this world. It is expected that one in four of all people over 65 years of age will require the services of a nursing home at some time during their life. Keep in mind that if, as occupants of nursing homes, they have spent themselves into being wards of the state after 22 months, they will have no resources left should they recover and no longer need the services of the nursing home. This happens more frequently than most people think. The Medicaid "spend down strategy" to finance nursing home expenses is not all it is cracked up to be on either an individual basis or a social basis.

Figure 2–4
Nursing Home Expenditures

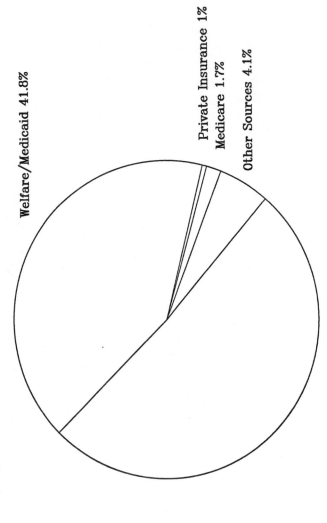

Welfare/Medicaid 41.8%

Private Insurance 1%
Medicare 1.7%
Other Sources 4.1%

Individual & Family 51.4%

Source: Health Care Financing Administration; Brookings Institution

A good solution to this problem is to have sufficient, continually replaceable, monthly income from pensions, social security and investments to adequately cover your potential nursing home need. Preferably, at least $36,000 per year, per person—about $100 per day. In today's world this would provide you sufficient income to afford a respectable nursing home without invading your principal. For those that have it, great! We needn't worry about you. For those who can accumulate it, go for it! But for those that don't have resources, a nursing home policy of some kind will be necessary to provide for some or all of these potential future needs. Typically, we don't like the thought of nursing homes or nursing home policies. We hope that we are among the 3 out of 4 who won't have to use one. However, a one in four risk is more than most of us or our families can afford.

Fortunately, the insurance industry is creating private policies that can reduce this worry and give the family some peace of mind. For example, my mother has given up $150 per month of her retirement income in premium payments to assure that if she ever needs to be an occupant of a nursing home, her insurance company will deliver $1,500 per month to her to help offset the expenses. She, and the rest of the family, are confident that her nursing home requirements could be met by the benefits provided by that policy and her own resources, and she would never have to be "spent down to Medicare." Representative nursing home policy rates are shown in Figure 2–5.

Figure 2–5 shows us that a typical couple, ages 65 and 62, purchasing a $100 per day policy with a 20-day elimination period and a 5-year benefit period, would be paying almost $2,600 per year ($1,440 + $1,152) for nursing home coverage. This would protect them against $36,500 of nursing home expenses for each person per year, a total exposure of $182,500 per person. We must recommend that they buy the policy if they do not have the resources to pay the $73,000 per year ($36,500 × 2) in nursing home expenses.

If this same couple had started planning one year earlier, they could have purchased a cash value nursing home policy for $1,500 each—$3,000 per year (See Figure 2–6), only $400

Figure 2-5

NURSING HOME POLICY
$100 Per Day
(1989 Rates)

No Prior Hospitalization Required

Annual Premiums

Duration of Benefits	Elimination Period			
	0 Days	20 Days	100 Days	150 Days
AGE 60				
One Year	$ 720	$ 600	$ 504	$ 456
Two Years	960	816	720	648
Three Years	1080	924	790	720
Five Years	1212	1044	912	840
AGE 62				
One Year	780	648	540	492
Two Years	1044	888	804	696
Three Years	1188	1020	864	792
Five Years	1332	1152	1008	924
AGE 65				
One Year	924	792	636	588
Two Years	1284	1092	936	852
Three Years	1464	1260	1056	972
Five Years	1668	1440	1236	1152
AGE 70				
One Year	1416	1212	960	888
Two Years	2028	1740	1428	1332
Three Years	2364	2028	1692	1548
Five Years	2724	2352	2004	1860

per year more than the non-cash value contract. The cash value provision makes nursing home policies more palatable to those who object to paying premiums for something on which they may never collect. It provides for a return of an increasing percentage of the premium paid of up to 100% at the 20th year. The percentage continues to increase beyond the 20th year. It is particularly appealing if you are just about to move into the next five-year age bracket. Warning—some cash value policies are available only with the 3-day hospitalization requirement. The 3-day hospitalization requirement makes them inappropriate for most people. Check the policy provisions carefully.

Today's long-term care policies, in spite of the fact that they are superior to those available in the marketplace as recently as 1987, are still not where they should be. There are too many "ifs" in long-term care policies. They will pay in some cases, if you are a resident of a nursing home, if the nursing home is "qualified," if you spent three days in the hospital before being admitted to the nursing home, and on and on. You will note that many of these "ifs" concern where an individual is being taken care of, not why.

People need assistance if they become functionally disabled; that is, they are unable to provide for their own daily nourishment, personal hygiene and safety. This need is not entirely addressed in disability income policies that replace a portion of income during your working years. Functional disability not only terminates income but adds the expenses of those required to perform the functions that the disabled individual cannot perform. Once your working years are over and you are living on capital, the typical disability income policy becomes irrelevant and is dropped, leaving you without protection for functional disability.

No matter what our age, we are all exposed to this problem. It is time that the insurance industry came up with a functional disability income rider! They should be able to define functional disability and to evaluate, with the help of a physician, whether a person is functionally disabled. If such a situation is certified to be the case by a doctor, then I would expect a functional disability income policy or rider to pay benefits based on the fact that I need assistance, not on where I choose to obtain it. A nursing home may be the logical place but, possibly as a result of personal circumstances, home health care may be a better and less expensive solution. Adult day care may be an even better solution. I hope that in the

Figure 2–6

NURSING HOME POLICY
$100 Per Day
(1989 Rates)

3–day Hospitalization Required

Annual Premiums

Duration of Benefits	Elimination Period			
	0 Days	20 Days	100 Days	150 Days
AGE 50–54				
One Year	$ 696	$ 600	$ 528	$ 504
Two Years	888	768	696	660
Three Years	996	864	780	756
Five Years	1128	972	912	876
AGE 55–59				
One Year	780	660	588	564
Two Years	1008	876	792	768
Three Years	1140	984	912	864
Five Years	1296	1128	1044	1008
AGE 60–64				
One Year	984	828	732	708
Two Years	1320	1128	1032	996
Three Years	1524	1308	1200	1140
Five Years	1728	1500	1404	1344
AGE 65–69				
One Year	1476	1212	1056	1008
Two Years	2064	1728	1560	1488
Three Years	2412	2016	1848	1752
Five Years	2784	2352	2196	2100

future we will find that adult foster care is the more humane and economical way to provide for some of our senior citizens. We are being forced to circumvent alternative care possibilities and institutionalize all the functionally disabled in nursing homes in order to receive payment from the insurance companies. This is an inhumane and unnecessarily expensive response to this problem.

However, we must deal with long-term care insurance as it is available today. The importance of this type of coverage is increasing with our aging population due to our ability to keep people alive. Hypertension, heart disease and diabetes have diminished as major killers and are now some of the major causes of disability. How many of us have seen our parents and/or grandparents disabled by a broken hip, loss of eyesight or hearing, which changes an otherwise independent person into one who suddenly is dependent? Legislation is needed to allow for the pre-funding of long-term care expenses in reserve funds that are not subject to current taxation. Functional disability riders would then become practical additions to a regular disability income policy as well as individual life insurance policies.

Some individual life insurance policies being issued today allow you to access your policy's cash value under certain circumstances. They are marketed as policies with "living benefits" that may serve as a substitute for a nursing home policy. They generally are unacceptable because they contain too many "ifs." In many cases, they read like the "dread disease" policies which are marketed by insurance companies preying upon people's fear of certain diseases, such as polio, cancer or AIDS. The policy pays benefits only if you are afflicted with that particular disease. Such policies are neither practical, economical nor appropriate. In order to build family security, you cannot accept policies that will protect you against one disease, but not another. Such policies enrich insurance companies but do little to provide you, the consumer, with adequate protection. You will find an Action Letter concerning the purchase of a nursing home insurance policy in Figure 2–7.

The third paragraph of this Action Letter gives the specifications that you want for a policy for your own use. It will be up to you to describe what you feel you need. The statistical averages indicate that the average nursing home in the United States costs approximately $24,000 per year, $66 per day, and that the average stay is two years. We recommend that you avoid considering yourself one of the statistical

Figure 2–7
Action Letter

Dear _____:

We need your assistance. We are in search of a quality nursing home policy and would appreciate it if you could provide us with quotes and information.

I was born _____ , and am a male/female, smoker/ non-smoker in good health. My spouse was born _____ , and is a male/female, smoker/non-smoker also in good health.

I would like quotes on guaranteed renewable long-term care policies providing benefits of _____ per day after an elimination period of _____ days, for a benefit period of at least _____ years. I would like to have the benefits payable regardless of whether the nursing home I use is classified, skilled, intermediate care, respite or a custodial care home. I would also like to have benefits payable if the required personal care is provided in our own home or in an adult day-care center. I wish to avoid any policies that have exclusions for Alzheimer's disease or organic brain disease of any sort, and policies which include pre-entry requirements such as the three day hospitalization requirement.

I would like to know of any pre-existing condition limitations, and the requirements for application. I would appreciate your recommendations in regard to any supplemental benefits the policy should offer, such as an inflation rider.

Please call me if you have any questions. I look forward to receiving your proposals in the mail so that I may review them with my advisor. We will then ask you to visit with us to respond to our questions. Thank you for your assistance.

Sincerely,

averages. Choose a cost-effective waiting period, determined by how long you could pay the bill yourself, and have benefits payable for at least a 5-year period. Your decision as to the amount to be paid for each day should be based upon the costs of facilities in your area that you would find acceptable, and your alternative resources. An inflation rider can be an important addition to the policy.

An example of the decision making process would be as follows. A typical couple in retirement is living on a combination of social security benefits, pension income and personal investment income. They would not need one of today's nursing home policies if they currently are living comfortably on the income being generated by these three sources (without invading principal), and if the income available would be entirely sufficient to cover the cost of care if they both, husband and wife, were functionally disabled. (Indeed, some individuals may be able to reside full time in a quality nursing facility without spending any more than what it costs them to live presently. Such individuals have no need to purchase nursing home policies.)

Another couple in the same situation may find that, although the present resources provide adequately for their chosen standard of living, nursing home expenses would indeed increase their cost of living and strain their capital resources. They could not live on the interest earnings of capital alone, but would have to spend their capital. They need a nursing home policy. They may say that their resources would support $50 per day in a nursing home, not $100 a day, the expected costs for them. In that event, it would be appropriate to purchase at least a $50 per day nursing home policy.

Suppose an individual had earnings of approximately $18,000 per year, and typical nursing home costs in the area were twice that, $36,000 per year. A $50 per day nursing home policy would, assuming the individual was about age 70, cost about $1200 per year, or for $100 per month. The question becomes, can $100 per month be taken out of current income to offset the potential loss that would occur in the event of admittance to a nursing home? If that retiree could not afford the policy, and yet would be likely to use up all of his assets and become dependent on others in the family, then others in the family might be eager to contribute to the $100 per month premium payment so that they would be protected against substantially higher costs should that relative become confined to a nursing facility.

The costs quoted in Figures 2–5 and 2–6 are for illustration purposes only. You will find that policies and costs differ from state to state depending upon the requirements that the state insurance commissioner has put on insurance companies issuing nursing home policies. There are substantial differences in regulations that have resulted in substantial difference in costs in some areas. You will find that sending the Action Letter will get you the factual data that you need in order to make an informed decision.

Another source of information regarding long-term care policies is your state insurance commissioner's office. This type of coverage has created a great deal of interest, and rapid changes in policies have resulted in much confusion and political involvement. State insurance commissioners throughout the country have been very sympathetic to the plight of people shopping for this type of policy and have, in many cases, put together studies designed to help them purchase good policies. Call your state insurance commissioner's office and ask for their help.

Summary

You might be tempted to ask at this point, "What is worse than disability?" The answer is, "Disability with no money." A quality disability income policy owned personally, which the insurance company cannot cancel or change other than as stated in the contract, is the solution to this problem during those years in which you work for a living. In some cases you will find that this is an impossible or an impractical solution because of your particular circumstances. The second best alternative is disability income insurance provided by a quality insurance company through your employer, with the stipulation that you pay income taxes on the entire premium so that benefits come to you without current income taxation. If this too is unavailable, then look to the associations and organizations of which you are a member for an association group plan to which you can belong.

We all strive for the point in life where we have accumulated sufficient social security benefits, pension and retirement benefits, and personal capital so that we continue to work for fun rather than out of necessity. When this day arrives, the disability income policy that you have owned, in order to provide for income needs in case your paycheck stopped, is no longer an economic necessity. If you cease to work, your income continues from your investments, pensions and social security in sufficient quantity to maintain your standard of living.

Your next need is for a functional disability policy, because if you are functionally disabled, the expenses of your long-term care could exceed what you require for maintaining your standard of living. If they do, your principle would be eroded, which would erode your income; eventually you would find yourself qualifying for Medicaid, which really wasn't your ambition in life. The solutions today are better than they ever have been. Take the time to find them, and get help.

THREE

MEDICAL EXPENSE HEALTH INSURANCE

The basic objective of medical expense insurance is to make sure that you and your family are never exposed to medical bankruptcy.

With this objective in mind, the first specification for a policy is that it have an "unlimited" maximum. That is not always possible and, in fact, it was more readily available between 1980 and 1988 than it is now. A number of major insurance companies no longer offer unlimited policies. They have reduced their maximums to one million dollars. Although the one million dollar maximum does sound like a significant amount, and it certainly is, that does not mean it is necessarily enough. Your strategy will be to go for the best, request the unlimited, and compromise only if you find that the best is unavailable or impractical.

Optimally, the policy should cover all physician-prescribed treatments to diagnose and correct a medical condition; the insurance company should pay those bills after an acceptable deductible; and you will participate in the payment of the bills up to some relatively small percentage, such as 20%, while the insurance company pays the other 80% of those bills. It is entirely possible that you could go medically bankrupt paying 20% of unlimited bills. As a result, you will want what we refer to as a "stop-loss provision" in order to obligate the insurance company to pay 100% of the bills for the balance of the calendar year. This serves to limit your out-of-pocket costs for medical expenses during any one calendar year for you and your family, which is the key to avoiding medical bankruptcy. It is important that you know how much would have to be paid out of your own pocket in the way of deductibles and co-insurance if you and others in your family suffered a number of severe illnesses in one year. Once you have determined the amount you can make sure that your emergency fund is built up to provide for this worst case scenario.

Unlimited maximum, comprehensive coverage, reasonable deductibles and an acceptable stop-loss; those are our specifications. However pre-existing conditions may be an obstacle you will have to face. When applying for insurance coverage with an individual policy, as opposed to group insurance, you will have to answer questions regarding your medical history. This will reveal anything that has happened in your past that would affect the insurance company's ability to provide health insurance for you profitably. On other policies, such as group insurance, you may not have to complete any medical questions, but the policy will state that it will not pay benefits for conditions that manifested themselves before the policy was put in force.

Pre-existing conditions may be excluded entirely or they may be excluded only for certain periods of time. In some cases, insurance companies will pay some benefits for pre-existing conditions but limit the amount of the total payments. Any condition that has been diagnosed by a physician should be revealed on the application. It does not pay to turn in fraudulent applications to insurance companies. When you file a claim for an unrevealed pre-existing condition, the insurance company will, and must, refuse to pay. You are much better off being candid and thorough with the insurance company, so that if and when they do issue a policy, you have reasonable assurance that the promised benefits will be paid and the policy will not be rescinded because of any erroneous or misleading statements on the application. It is essential that you be very honest with the insurance professional with whom you are working, so that he can find the best source for your health insurance.

Many policies today contain inside limits that restrict the benefits that are payable for a number of conditions. Limits on benefits paid for mental or nervous disorders, and also drug and alcohol problems, are common. Insurance companies have found that bills for these types of problems frequently are unending. Conditions which are difficult to diagnose and difficult to treat with measurable results are often excluded within a policy and/or subject to limits on what the insurer will pay. You will want to check these carefully with your professional so that your policy does not present you with any unpleasant surprises.

Sources of Health Insurance

We previously suggested that your keystone disability insurance policy be a personally owned policy which the insurance company guarantees you can keep for the whole of your working life. It also should guarantee that there will be no change in costs or benefits other than as stated in the contract at issue. Seek such a policy first; and to the extent that it is not available or contains insufficiencies, supplement it with other coverage. If a medical insurance policy with these same provisions was available, I would suggest the same thing. However, no one issues a comprehensive medical insurance policy in which the benefits and the costs are guaranteed at the date of issue and thereafter cannot be changed. There are health policies which are guaranteed renewable, meaning that the insurance company cannot cancel or change the policy benefits once it is issued, however, the insurance company does reserve the right to change the cost of the policy on what they refer to as a class basis. This means that all people with similar policies would be exposed to the same cost increase at the same time. In effect, the insurance company would not select you *individually* for a rate increase.

The keystone coverage in the medical insurance field is your employer provided policy. If you have access to an employer provided medical insurance policy, it is highly likely that the employer is subsidizing it substantially or, in some rare cases, paying the entire premium for you on that policy. The advantage to this arrangement is that you need not report what the employer pays for that policy as taxable income as long as the employer is treating all employees equally. The employer also is allowed to deduct the cost as an employee benefit. This makes the employer the efficient purchaser of medical insurance from an income tax standpoint. Even with group policies, more and more insurance companies are demanding medical background before approving the coverage, a trend that will soon bring about further regulation.

Medical insurance plans usually are one of four types; Indemnity plans, Service Provider plans, Preferred Provider plans or Health Maintenance Organizations.

Indemnity Plans

After you have experienced a loss, indemnity plans reimburse you for that particular loss in accordance with the policy provisions. Indemnity plans offer the insured the advantage of selecting his or her own physician and/or hospital. You may choose the best, and the best may also be the most expensive—this has been the problem with the indemnity plan. The giver of care and the receiver of care have no personal incentive to keep costs reasonable. Consequently, costs have gotten out of hand. Recent medical insurance plans have been designed to involve both the recipient and the care-giver in providing cost-efficient medical care and, in this way, to bring down the costs for all.

Figure 3–1 shows the circle of payments relating to medical conditions. The diagram depicts the employee/patient /customer pouring in the dollars, and the provider, eventually receiving the dollars. You are that employee/patient/customer! With the indemnity plan, the employee knows that the bill will be paid in accordance with the plan's provisions and therefore does not particularly care what the treatment costs. The provider is not answerable to anyone but the patient in spite of the fact that it will be either the government, the insurance company or the employer (self-insured plan) that will pay that provider. The provider's only interest is providing top-quality medical treatment and, theoretically, he has the unlimited resources of the insurance company, government or the employer to pay for those services. The resulting skyrocketing costs of indemnity plans are being paid by *you* through higher product prices, higher costs, deductibles and co-insurance or lower wage increases.

Figure 3–1   **WHO DOES PAY?**

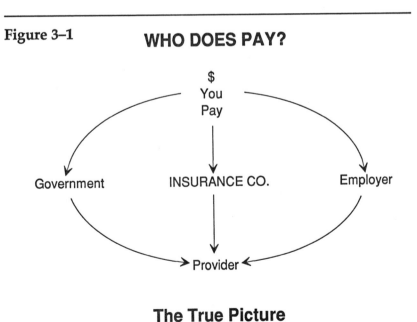

The True Picture

Service Provider Plans

Blue Cross/Blue Shield service organizations offered some of the first "fee for service" types of plans in which the insurance organization tried also to be the provider of care. Blue Cross/Blue Shield provides their participants with the facilities of the member hospitals and physicians for a monthly subscriber's fees. If the insurance company and the provider are one and the same, the insurance company maintains cost control. Theoretically, this makes them better able to estimate the charge to subscribers. Many Blue Cross organizations contract with the hospital to provide the benefits required by its plan. Since it is supplying that provider with a substantial amount of business, it will negotiate discounted rates whether that provider is a doctor or a hospital. However, in other Blue Cross organizations, the hospital is owned by Blue Cross, making it similar to a Health Maintenance Organization.

Preferred Provider Plans

Preferred Provider Organizations (PPO) are arrangements established by commercial insurance companies following the Blue Cross/Blue Shield example. Coalitions of insurance companies will negotiate with providers to obtain discounted rates for the insureds and then guarantee patients to that provider. You will be encouraged to use these providers by means of lower deductibles, lower co-insurance and, in some cases, less paperwork than if you went to a provider outside of the PPO network.

Health Maintenance Organizations

Health Maintenance Organizations (HMO) are assemblages of physicians and hospitals joined together in one business arrangement. In effect they state to their members that they will "maintain their health" for a stipulated amount of money per month. Kaiser Permanenti in California is an example of one of the oldest and best managed health maintenance organizations in the country.

All of these arrangements work well if they are economically sound and if you are in fairly good health.. However, if either of these factors deteriorate, the whole system may deteriorate. In 1989, a major Health Maintenance Organization went into Chapter 11, leaving hundreds of thousands of people in doubt about their coverage. Imagine how members of this organization felt if their health was failing at the same time!

Recently the government has been managing health care costs simply by not paying any hospital or doctor bills that they deem to be too high. In the case of Medicaid, when the state runs out of money the bills go unpaid. As you might expect, that's a bit rough on the providers, and is the reason you've read about the economic failure of some hospitals. Such failures are particularly hard on the poor because many of these hospitals were trying to provide health care for those of limited means.

Those living in rural areas are even more at risk of having their hospitals close than those people living in urban areas. According to a Senate Aging Committee report released in October of 1988, Medicare, in its infinite wisdom, pays rural hospitals 14.5% less than it pays urban hospitals for the same services to Medicare patients. According to this report, over 20% of our country's 2,700 rural hospitals face closing in the years ahead. Government bureaucrats with little medical background find themselves in supervisory positions over physicians and hospitals. In spite of their good intentions, they have driven good physicians into retirement and allowed bad physicians to flourish with exorbitant profits.

Private Industry

What about private industry? How good are private insurance companies at managing health care? In the preferred provider organization management is primarily through what they call a "gatekeeper" physician or "quarterback" doctor. ALL your physician services will be delivered through this physician. If you need a specialist, this gatekeeper will assign that specialist; and if that specialist wants to take an X-ray, he will ask permission of your gatekeeper to do so. If the organization providing your care works properly, and all participants are confident in each other's fairness, permission will be granted for your X-ray. However, don't be surprised if the gatekeeper doctor demands that the request for the X-ray be in writing and insists on responding to that request in writing, a process which could delay your X-ray 10 days or more. This is what happens when your providers find themselves in adversary relationships with each other and with the insurance company sponsoring the PPO. When this occurs, the patient or the patient's family must get involved by contacting the patient's hotline (which is normally available) and finding a superior who will facilitate matters. Needless to say, the managed care concept of delivering health care is just developing, and is practicied by more unqualified people that the industry would care to admit. It will take more time and patience than most of us possess before it will work well.

One alternative offered by many commercial insurance companies is the combination indemnity plan/PPO option. Under this arrangement, the insured employee does not commit to the indemnity or the PPO plan in advance, but decides which to use at the time care is needed. The employer will attempt to steer the employee toward the PPO by means of lower deductibles and lower co-insurance than are available under the indemnity plan, but it is ultimately the employee's choice. If the care is needed for something the employee feels can and will be handled well by the PPO, the PPO would be the choice. However, if the employee has a rare disease, for which there are few qualified specialists available, the indemnity plan would allow the patient to select the provider of choice. This flexibility is a distinct advantage and is our choice among the alternatives. The HMO alternative can be extremely tempting because the benefits are often delivered without annoying paperwork and with low, or no, deductibles and co-insurance. Indeed, an HMO staffed by high-quality, capable, caring physicians with excellent facilities and strong finances would be ideal—too bad they are so few and far between!

An HMO that has money problems is not an adequate alternative. As funds get low, good doctors leave, good staff is cut and the more expensive procedure or tests are not ordered. If you happen to be a patient with substantial medical problems in this situation, you have problems! It is highly unlikely that you can know the financial strength of an independent HMO. We have seen patients suffer as HMOs became insolvent. An independent HMO is not the provider I would choose as the sole provider of care anymore than I would an insurance company that is not financially sound.

Who Pays for Health Care?

You will note in Figure 3–1 the dollar signs and arrows showing funds coming from your pockets—the citizen/employee/patient—through government, through the insurance company and through employers to eventually reach the pockets of the providers. In one nonsensical survey, respondents were asked who should pay for the increase in cost of health insurance: themselves, the government, insurance companies, or their employer. As you might expect, no one voted the increased costs to themselves. Most suggested that it would be a good idea for government or employers to pay the increased costs. Keep in mind as you go about solving your own medical insurance problems that only *people* pay medical bills. They may pay for it directly to the provider, through an insurance company in the way of insurance premium, through their employer as a result of reduced wages or higher prices for goods and services, or through the government in the way of taxes. It's all *your* money. The inefficiencies of the various conduits that carry dollars from your pockets to those of the providers merely add to your cost.

Also, as you consider the health insurance alternatives, keep in mind that if you choose a plan that locks you into a specific organization, hospital or group of physicians, and will not pay outside of that group, you are then entirely dependent upon the quality of those doctors to solve any medical problems you might have. Choose such a plan wisely.

COBRA

On April 7, 1986, the Consolidated Omnibus Budget Reconciliation Act (COBRA) was enacted. It is applicable to employers providing health benefits to groups of 20 or more employees. It allows employees to continue group insurance, in most cases, even after employment has terminated. The employee pays the full cost of what the employer was paying for the plan and possibly up to 2% more for administrative expenses. For a qualified employee, the continuation may extend up to 18 months. Spouses and children may have up to 36 months of continued health insurance. As a rule of thumb, if you qualify, sign up. Don't ever go even one day without health insurance.

The COBRA provisions are a boon to terminating employees and dependents since they make health insurance available regardless of physical condition. However, premium payments to continue the coverage must be made promptly. Estimates show that it is costing employers $2 for each $1 a continuing employee or dependent pays in premium under COBRA. As a result, employers have been advised to terminate employees' COBRA coverage if they don't pay their premiums on time, so don't be late!

Conversion

In many states, your final chance to continue your health insurance without having to requalify medically would come at the end you your COBRA benefits, at which time you may have the right to convert to an individual policy. Typically, these conversion policies are relatively expensive and the benefits are very restrictive. The conversion privileges, therefore, are of value to those who cannot obtain health insurance in any other way.

All information about employer provided medical insurance should be readily available to you in booklets and descriptive pamphlets. If you have trouble extracting the important information from those materials, you can use the "Action Letter" to medical insurance providers (Figure 3–2) that asks the most important questions for you. Try recording the information you want by going through the booklets yourself and filling in the blanks in the letter. If this does not work, the letter is designed to be sent to your insurance provider or benefits manager. They should be able to provide you with the information.

Individual Medical Insurance

If employer provided health insurance is not a viable alternative, you will apply directly to an insurance company for an individually issued policy. The advantage of this procedure is that you can more of less dictate the type of benefits you want. The disadvantage is that you have no employer to help you pay for the insurance. Unfortunately, individual insurance is most readily available if you are healthy. In applying for an individual health insurance policy, the insurance company will ask you a dizzying array of medical questions. They will want to know the personal health history of you and everyone in your family. It is in your best interest to divulge everything because even if you have a particular health condition that the insurance company might not wish to cover, they may be able to issue the policy with an exclusion rider. The policy would cover everything but that particular condition, certainly a better alternative than no health insurance at all. Another advantage of an individual policy is the availability of a guaranteed renewable contract, which prohibits the insurance company from cancelling your policy, but allows it to adjust the costs for the insurance as long it does so on a class basis. Many people opt to purchase an individually issued, guaranteed renewable health insurance policy to gain more control over the continuation of their personal health insurance. Choosing a high deductible can keep

Figure 3–2
Employee Benefit Medical Insurance Action Letter

I would appreciate your assistance in evaluating my medical insurance.

I have listed below the specific information I would like regarding my medical insurance. Please feel free to fill in the answers on this letter and return it to me.

1. Maximum limit on the total benefit payments _____

2. Individual deductible amount _____

3. Limit on deductible for a family _____

4. Co-insurance provision: I pay _____

              Insurance company pays _____

5. Stop loss provision: per individual _____

                      per family_____

6. Duration of stop loss _____

7. Any interior limits I should be aware of? _____

Please send me any descriptive material you have on the plan along with claim forms and instructions

I look forward to hearing from you. Thank you for your assistance.

Sincerely,

the cost down, and the guaranteed renewability assures them that they can keep the policy in force as long as they want to pay the billed premiums.

The Action Letter to request quotes regarding private health insurance (Figure 3–3) first lists the specifics regarding those who need health insurance (dates of birth, smoker or non-smoker, health conditions) for all members of the family. It then requests a comprehensive major medical policy that is guaranteed renewable throughout your lifetime and has an unlimited lifetime maximum. You then select an appropriate deductible. You can ask the insurance professional to provide you with quotes at various deductibles so that you may choose the one that is most cost-effective for you. It states your requested co-insurance provision—that is, how much of the initial billing you would pay and how much the insurance company would pay, stipulating the most typical split, 80%/20%. The letter next asks for your maximum out-of-pocket exposure so that you will know what medical bills could be under a worst-case scenario. It also asks for a full explanation of any inside limits for things such as drug-, alcohol- or mental health-related conditions. This letter again asks for quotes from a number of different insurance companies and for the professional's recommendation as to which one he thinks would serve you best.

Association Medical Insurance

Another alternative for obtaining medical insurance may be through an association of which you are a member. Many such organizations provide their members with various forms of insurance. Some of the organizations sell the insurance just to provide an extra benefit for their membershp; others in order to make a profit for their organization. You obviously would prefer the former. What you seek, of course, is comprehensive coverage such as that described in the following Action Letter. Some of the less savory fare offered up by associations are policies that pay you a stipulated amount of money each day you are in the hospital. Keep in mind that

Figure 3–3
Individual Medical Insurance Action Letter

Dear Sir:

I am in need of private medical insurance. I am male/female born
_____ . I am a smoker/non-smoker in excellent/good/fair health.

My spouse is a male/female born _____ and is a smoker/non-smoker in excellent/good/fair health.

We have/do not have children. Their names, dates of birth, sex and basic health condition are listed on the back of this letter.

I would like a comprehensive major medical policy that is Lifetime Guaranteed Renewable and has an Unlimited Lifetime Maximum.

Other plan features are:

1. Individual deductible $100/$200/$500/$1,000/$2,000/$_____ .

2. Co-Insurance Provision 80/20 (Insurance company pays 80%, I pay 20%)

3. STOP-Loss Provision — What is my maximum out-of-pocket requirement?
   For the family _____
   For how long _____

Please send me quotes from _____ companies including any descriptive material you have on the plans along with enrollment forms and instructions.

I would appreciate your evaluation of the coverages regarding which one you feel is fairly priced and sufficiently comprehensive to provide for my family.

If you have any questions, please call me at _____ . I look forward to hearing from you. Thank you for your assistance.

Sincerely,

the average stay in the hospital is less than 10 days, and a $50 per day indemnity policy paying you $500 is not going to be much help. Also, beware of policies that will pay benefits only if your medical condition is caused by an accident or some specific illness or illnesses. They are cheap policies, but not as cheap as they ought to be. They are a high-profit item to the insurance companies issuing them. Avoid them: obtain high-quality comprehensive coverage instead.

Federal Government Provided Medical Insurance

Government is the final source of medical coverage. Both federal and state governments provide medical insurance benefits. The Medicare program of the Federal Government provides mandatory basic hospitalization benefits for most U.S. citizens over the age of 65 and some other special classes of individuals. This coverage, referred to as Part A, is supplemented by Part B of Medicare which is a voluntary program that provides for the payment of doctor bills. All eligible individuals should sign up for these plans three months prior to their 65th birthday. A summary of the benefits provided under the Medicare Catastrophic Coverage Act of 1988 is shown in Figure 3–4. These plans are normally insufficient by themselves, and it is recommended that a supplemental plan be purchased.

Medicare Supplement Insurance—Medigap

The primary reason for a Medigap policy is the need for coverage for that portion of the doctor bill that Medicare deems "excessive." It was reported in the June 1989 issue of *Consumer Reports* (an issue in which Trudy Lieberman provides an outstanding study of Medigap policies and your need for them) that excess charges averaged 37% more than Medicare allowable charges. *You* pay 100% of the excess! A doctor who accepts only what Medicare allows is a "participating" physician; others are "non-participating" physicians. About one out of every three physicians are par-

Figure 3-4
Medicare Catastrophic Coverage Act 1988

Inpatient Hospital Care

Days Covered	Unlimited per year
Deductible	One per year estimated at $564 in 1989
Copayments	None

Physician & Other Outpatient Services

Deductible/Copayment	$75 per year/20% of reasonable charges A $1,370 annual cap begins in 1990
Charges Exceeding Medicare Limits	Patient pays all charges that are considered "unreasonable" by Medicare

Skilled Nursing Home Care

Days Covered	150 days per year
Copayments	$25.50 per day for the first 8 days
Prior Hospitalization	Not required

Prescription Drugs
1990 Medicare covers some intravenous therapy drugs used first year after transplantation. 20% copayment for immunosuppressives and $550 annual deductible for both drugs. Starting 1991 all outpatient drugs approved by the Food & Drug Administration. 1991: Deductible - $600, Copayment - 50%; 1992: Deuctible - $652, Copayment - 40%; 1993: Deductible - $710, Copayment - 20%.

Respite Care   80 hours per year

Home Health Care   Up to 38 days of care per illness, 7 days per week

Hospice Care   Up to 210 days of care with extensions beyond 210 days where recertified terminally ill

Mammogram   Covers mammogram every other year

Cost and Projected Costs

Part B Premium	1989: $31.10	1992: $52.60
(per month/per person)	1990: $36.00	1993: $62.80
	1991: $43.40	
Supplemental premium	1989: $22.50, cap $800	1992: $40.50, cap $950
as part of federal tax *	1990: $37.50, cap $850	1993: $42.00, cap $1,050
*(per year/per person)**	1991: $39.00, cap $900	

---

* (Determined by dividing the beneficiary's tax liability for the year by $150, then multiplying that number by the supplemental premium rate for the year. These rates are being reconsidered by Congress.)

ticipating. It is probable that this number will fall as Medicare continues its cutbacks. When Medicare refuses to pay it becomes impossible for these physicians to maintain their practices.

You can obtain a good Medigap policy for approximately $80 per month. You should be able to locate one by consulting the June 1989 *Consumers Report* article or your local insurance professional. But only one plan please—multiple Medigap policies are a waste of money. Your Medigap Action Letter is show in Figure 3–5.

State Government Insurance

Frequently, the state also offers insurance benefits via Medicaid that provide medical benefits to the indigent. The State of Illinois Medicaid pays the hospital only 62 cents for every dollar the Medicaid system is billed, leaving, the providers holding the bag for the rest, over one billion dollars in 1988.

A number of states have started catastrophic medical pools to provide insurance benefits for those uninsurable citizens who cannot get insurance in any other way. In order to find out about state insurance pools, contact your state insurance department and ask them to send you complete information and enrollment materials. The existence and the adequacy of such plans depends upon the economic health of the state in which you are a resident. For example, Illinois' Comprehensive Health Insurance plan (CHIP) was to start up on August 15, 1988, but as a result of lack of funding it did not begin until April of 1989.

The availability of medical insurance varies a great deal from location to location. It is constantly changing. It is strongly recommended that you work with a local insurance professional as you seek to obtain and evaluate adequate medical insurance. They know where quality coverage can be obtained for you.

Figure 3–5
Medigap Action Letter

Dear Sir:

I am in need of private Medigap insurance. I am a male/female born _____. I am a smoker/non-smoker in excellent/good/health.

My spouse is a male/female born _____ and is a smoker/non-smoker in excellent/good/fair health.

I would like a comprehensive medigap policy that is lifetime guaranteed renewable and has an unlimited lifetime maximum.

Other plan features desired are:

1. Cost-effective benefits that fill in the gaps by paying what Medicare parts A and B commonly exclude.
2. Usual and customary expense coverage so that the medigap policy will pay the excess charges between the usual and customary costs and the more limited Medicare-eligible expenses.

Please send me quotes from _____ companies including any descriptive material you have on the plans along with enrollment forms and instructions.

I would appreciate your evaluation of the coverages regarding which one you feel is fairly priced and sufficiently comprehensive to provide for my family.

If you have any questions, please call me at _____. I look forward to hearing from you. Thank you for your assistance.

Sincerely,

Summary

Now that we have explored the alternatives, it is time to take inventory of your own policy. Figure 3–6 will assist you in recording the essential information regarding your medical insurance and its costs. Does your policy meet the specifications of the policy we recommend? Unlimited maximum, reasonable deductibles and co-insurance, a stop-loss provision and only a few acceptable inside limits? If not, send the appropriate action letter to your medical insurance professional.

Figure 3–6
Medical & Dental Insurance

Insured	Company	Policy Number	Policy Maximum	Deductible	Co-Insurance	Stop-Loss	Remarks
1	___	___	___	___	___	___	___
2	___	___	___	___	___	___	___
3	___	___	___	___	___	___	___
4	___	___	___	___	___	___	___
5	___	___	___	___	___	___	___

Total Annual Family Premium: ___

FOUR

RESIDENCE/REAL ESTATE INSURANCE

Our objective in this chapter is to make sure that you have adequate insurance coverages related to where you live and what you own. If you already have a homeowner's or renter's policy, we need to find the essential information within that policy. Once you have completed the inventory shown in Figure 4–1, you will want to evaluate your coverage and determine if there is any way to improve the situation.

In order to complete the inventory, turn to the declarations page of your policy. Usually a new declarations page will be sent to you each year when you renew your policy. There you will find the information required in the inventory regarding the insurance company providing the coverage and the particular piece or pieces of real estate that are covered. It will also list the various insurance amounts that are provided, the premiums for those amounts and the time period during which the policy is in force. (Make a photocopy of the declara-

Figure 4-1
Residence/Real Estate Insurance Inventory

Company/ Real Estate	Liability Maximum	Medical Payment	Property Insurance Maximum	Policy Type	Special Riders	Policy Number	Annual Premium
1	___	___	___	___	___	___	___
2	___	___	___	___	___	___	___

Total Real Estate Annual Premium: ___

tions page because you will be using it later with an Action Letter.)

From the inventory of coverages, record the maximums for liability, medical payments, the amount for which the property is insured, the policy type, any special riders on the policy, the policy number and the annual premium. This format will work well for those with individual ownership of free-standing private property. You will have to adjust the format slightly if you rent your residence or live in a condominium or cooperative residence.

Figure 4–2 is your Real Estate Action Letter. It specifies what you want in coverage for your residence and other real estate holdings. Generally, we recommend that you send these specifications to your property/casualty insurance professional regardless of what you find on the inventory that you have completed. Since it is entirely possible that the maximum amount the insurance company will issue today is higher than what you were able to purchase when you originally obtained the policy, it is prudent to send this written request for a quote on the maximum amount of insurance currently available. In most cases, you will find that the cost differential to increase your policy from its present levels to the maximum coverage that the insurance company will provide are so minor that it doesn't make economic sense to have less than they will issue. It also gives your property/casualty agent an opportunity to review your coverage to make sure it conforms to the specifications in the Action Letter and is up-to-date, even if he disagrees with the specifications in the letter. In the following pages, we will examine each coverage offered in typical real estate insurance policies, the coverage recommended to you, and why.

Real Estate Liability

You will want to maximize your liability coverage. You have liability insurance because you, or a member of your family, may make a mistake that injures another. The law requires that people behave as reasonable and prudent individuals and

Figure 4–2
Real Estate Action Letter

Dear _____:

Please provide me with a quote on my Residence/Real Estate insurance coverage based on the following parameters:

1. Maintain my liability at the maximum amount available. I would like no less than $300,000, or the amount that would best coordinate with a personal umbrella liability policy.
2. Make sure that the coverage is of the comprehensive all-risk variety. I would like the most comprehensive, including coverage for personal property losses and indirect losses resulting from the loss of use of personal property.
3. Loss payments are to be made on a "replacement cost" basis rather than an "actual cash value" depreciated value basis for all coverages including personal property.
4. Please let me know if there are any discounts available for the following:

	I HAVE	DO NOT HAVE
Smoke Detectors	_____	_____
Fire Extinguishers	_____	_____
Deadbolt Locks	_____	_____
Other Protective Devices	_____	_____

5. Do I require any special coverages for household domestic help and/or other occasional workers hired for household work?
6. Please recommend cost-effective deductibles.
7. Please maximize guest medical.
8. Please let me know the cost of earthquake and/or flood coverage and your recommendations regarding my need for such coverage.
9. Do I have coverage for sewer back-up and sump pump failure?
10. Special items of value that should be included on a personal property rider are as follows:

Item	Value	Appraisal Method/Date
_____	_____	_____
_____	_____	_____

11. Do you recommend any Business Pursuits Endorsements?

encl. Copy of Declarations Page of Existing Insurance.

if you do not, this can constitute negligence. If that negligence leads to the injury of another individual, or the property of another individual, the negligent party may be held liable for damages. You will be held liable for your own actions but also may be held liable for the actions of your relatives who are residents in your household. You may be held liable for the action of a resident in your household who is under age 21 and in your care or that of someone else who is a resident of your home. You may be held liable for the animals for which you are legally responsible and also for the negligent operation of your insured, unlicensed vehicles which are used with your consent. Take a mental inventory of your household. How many people are you responsible for? Do any of them do things that you would not describe as reasonable and prudent, or more importantly, that your neighbor would not describe as reasonable and prudent? Do you have any animals that could cause someone injury? What about toys, bikes, boats, all-terrain vehicles, snowmobiles, and so on? What about equipment such as the lawnmower and the snowblower? Do you allow others to use any of your possessions, on your own insured property or, more hazardous still, off your own insured property?

You need to know how your policy will protect you from economic loss in any circumstance where you may be held responsible. You need to know the difference in protection that you have if unlicensed vehicles are insured and operated on your property with your consent, as opposed to the degree of protection that you have if they are operated on property other than your own. Ask your property liability insurance professional about liability suits that he knows of where homeowner's policies were not effective in providing protection. The bottom line is, don't risk a lot for a little. The "little" is the little additional premium you will pay when you ask for the maximum amount on the most comprehensive type of liability coverage.

Complete the inventory in Figure 4–1 with the name of your insurance company, the real estate insured and the liability maximum provided by your current policy. You will note in the Action Letter in Figure 4–2 that we have asked that the liability maximum be increased to the maximum amount practical when coordinated with your umbrella or comprehensive liability policy. In the chapter on liability insurance, we recommend that you obtain an umbrella liability policy or a comprehensive personal liability policy coordinated with your other property casualty insurances. The cost of such a policy is frequently related to the quantity and quality of your underlying property/casualty insurances. By telling your agent that you will be purchasing an umbrella liability policy, he can evaluate the increases in costs resulting from increasing your underlying policy and compare those increased costs with the resulting decreased cost of the umbrella policy. The coordination of the two should provide the most cost effective package for you.

Real Estate Medical Payments Coverage

Next record the medical payments provision amount shown in your real estate policy, on the inventory in Figure 4–1. The medical payment provision protects you by requiring that the insurer pay all reasonable medical expenses, including funeral expenses, incurred by persons who are injured while on your premises with your permission (or permission from someone else who is also covered by your policy). It will also pay if someone is injured away from your premises but their injury results from your activity or from the activities of someone insured under your policy. The medical payments provision will not pay benefits to you or your other insureds. It is to reimburse others for injuries related to the real estate. Frequently, we find the amount of insurance provided under this provision to be $1,000, since this is the basic limit for medical payments under a homeowner's policy. We all know that $1,000 will not go very far in covering medical bills today. Again, in the Action Letter, we have asked your agent to maximize your medical payments provision. You will probably find that the additional cost is not significant. Don't take a chance by rationalizing that everyone has medical coverage. Over 37 million people in the United States do *not* have medical insurance, and the number is increasing rather than decreasing. If the person making a claim against you is uninsured, they have no one other than you to look for reimbursement. We repeat, don't risk a lot for a little—*maximize*.

Real Property Loss

The next section on the inventory asks you to record your property insurance maximum from your declarations page. When dealing with the amount you will be reimbursed under your policy as a result of property destruction, refer to Figure 4–3 which describes the various types of homeowner's policies generally available. The property insurance maximum is referred to as the Dwelling Coverage or Coverage A under your policy and indicates the maximum the insurance company will pay in the event of the total destruction of your property. Do not relate the adequacy of the amount recorded to the market value of your home. Some seem to think that the land on which the home sits represents 20% of the market value and, since it cannot be destroyed, 80% of market value is the appropriate level of insurance coverage. This is a common error. The insurance company relates property coverage to the replacement cost of your property. The amount recorded should adequately cover 100% of the replacement cost of your home. If it does not, and your home is totally destroyed, the insurance company will not pay more than the amount stipulated under Coverage A unless your policy includes a valuable rider that may be referred to as an inflation guard endorsement. In that case you would, by paying a premium, make the insurance company responsible for keeping your coverage at 100% of replacement cost.

In determining replacement costs, the insurance company will ask you for information about the construction of your home and its location. Typically they will inspect the home and/or request pictures of it. They will use this information, along with information in their data banks regarding construction costs in your particular area, to estimate a replacement cost figure for you, recommend that you insure your home for that amount, and add an inflation guard endorsement to your policy. If their estimate of the replacement cost of your home proves inaccurate at the time of your loss, it will be the insurance company's responsibility to make up the difference, not yours. As a result of having the proper coverage in the event of the total destruction of your home, you will more likely have the proper coverage in the event of partial losses. For example, a fire that causes a $20,000 loss to a home that has a replacement value of $100,000 and is fully insured for that amount would pay the full amount of the $20,000 loss less the policy deductible.

The 80% Rule

There is an 80% rule that applies to partial losses. This rule states that a $20,000 claim would be fully paid even if this $100,000 home was insured for only $80,000 or 80% of its true replacement cost. However, what would happen if the owner of this home was risking a lot to save a little and had the home insured for only $40,000? Under these circumstances, the insurance company would not pay the entire loss but would share the loss with the insured. The amount the insurance company would pay would be related to the amount of insurance required to receive full reimbursement, $80,000 (on the $100,000 house), to the amount of insurance this homeowner chose to carry, $40,000. Since the insured was carrying one-half the amount of insurance required, the insurance company would reimburse for one-half the loss ($10,000 of the $20,000 loss) less the applicable policy deductible. Make sure that this does not happen to you. Your Action Letter will help by asking your property insurance professional to make sure that your home is insured at 100% of replacement cost, and includes the inflation guard endorsement.

Personal Property

Your Action Letter asks that your coverage be of the most comprehensive, all-risk variety available for property, personal property and indirect losses resulting from loss of personal property. You want to be insured against all the risks the insurance company will possibly insure you against, however you also want to discuss the cost-effectiveness of the riders that provide this coverage. The premium effectiveness question comes up twice—once when you are paying the premium and once when you are making a claim, with 20/20 hindsight. The basic rules are, "Don't trade dollars with the insurance company," and "Self-insure small frequent losses."

Figure 4-3
Homeowners Coverage—Section One

	100% Dwelling Coverage A	10% of a Other Structures Coverage B	50% of a Personal Property Coverage C	20% of a Loss of Use Coverage D
HO–1	Basic	Basic	Basic	Basic (10% of A)
HO–2	Broad	Broad	Broad	Broad
HO–3	All Risk	All Risk	Broad*	All Risk
HO–4 (For Renters)	Not Applicable	Not Applicable	Broad (Basic Coverage)	Broad (20% of C)
HO–5	All Risk	All Risk	All Risk	All Risk
HO–6 (For Condo Dwellers)	Not Applicable	Not Applicable	Broad	Broad (40% of C)
HO–8 (For Properties Not Qualifying for HO–1, 2, 3, or 5)	Basic (ACV only)	Basic	Basic	Basic

* HO—15 Converts Broad to modified All Risk.

The "HO" Puzzle

Figure 4–3 illustrates the various varieties of homeowner's coverage. The diagram refers to various policy types, HO-1 through HO-6 and HO-8, that provide differing levels of coverage for various types of residences. If you have an HO-1 policy, all you have is basic coverage. The HO-1 type of policy was the first of the homeowner's series and provides protection against only the specific perils listed such as, fire and lightning, vandalism, malicious mischief, glass breakage, theft and volcanic eruption—i.e., basic coverage.

The HO-2 policy which improved upon the HO-1, is called broad form coverage. The HO-2 policy includes all the perils named in the HO-1 and adds six more: it also covers losses caused by falling objects; weight of ice, snow and sleet; heating or air conditioning system damage; water damage; frozen plumbing; and injury by artificially generated electricity. It also eliminates the exclusion under the HO-1 policy for smoke damage from fireplaces. You will find many HO-2 policies still in existence today.

Probably the most cost-effective homeowner's policy today is the HO-3 policy that pays benefits for all losses except those specifically excluded by the policy. It does not define the specific perils for which the policy will pay benefits, as do HO-1 and HO-2. HO-3 is referred to as "open perils" or "all-risk" coverage and it applies to the dwelling, the *other structures* and *loss of use*. The other structures provision provides an amount of insurance equal to 10% of the amount on the dwelling itself for other detached structures on the property, such as a garage. The loss of use coverage provides funds up to 20% of the amount of coverage on the dwelling to pay any outside living expenses required as a result of the loss.

The *personal property* coverage under an HO-3 policy provides for payments up to an amount equal to 50% of the coverage on the dwelling to reimburse you for losses caused to your personal property. Personal property coverage is on a broad form, rather than an all-risk basis. This coverage for personal property may be extended by various riders but, in order to get true all-risk coverage for personal property, you may find that you have to pay a great deal more than you are willing to pay. The high cost results from the fact that all-risk coverage to personal property may include the risk of your own personal carelessness, which can mean frequent claims. Thus, this coverage can become very expensive and possibly impractical.

The highest quality homeowner's policy is the HO-5 policy. It provides all-risk coverage for the dwelling, the other structures, personal property and loss of use. This policy is available only in limited circumstances. You may find that your insurance agent cannot provide it for you. When it is available it is relatively expensive, but it is the most comprehensive policy.

Riders and Endorsements

The standard provisions under the homeowner's coverage relating to what will be paid for other structures (10%), personal property (50%) and loss of use (20%), may be inadequate for you. You may increase the coverage by purchasing riders and/or endorsements to your policy. You are advised to purchase the *replacement cost* endorsement mentioned in the Action Letter so that reimbursements will be made on a replacement cost basis rather than on an actual cash value/depreciated value basis for all coverages, including personal property. Unless you have requested this replacement cost coverage, the policy will contain provisions relating to reimbursing you on an *actual cash value* basis of your lost property. Actual cash value means that your reimbursement for losses will be made on the basis of current replacement cost less depreciation. For example, if your five-year old TV set is destroyed and it will cost you $600 to replace it today, the insurance company may say that the set has depreciated at the rate of 10% per year. You may receive a check for $300, less your deductible, instead of being reimbursed $600 for its loss. In order to avoid this problem, the replacement cost rider assures indemnification for the full replacement cost of the item without any deduction for depreciation at the time of the loss.

The personal property reimbursement section of your homeowner's policy will have interior limits on the amount that it may reimburse you for certain items. Figure 4–4 provides a list of those personal property limitations.

In examining Figure 4–4, you may find that you own certain items that cannot be adequately provided for within the limitations. Inventory those items such as jewelry, silverware, firearms, etc. with appraisals and request that a rider or endorsement to your policy be provided in order to provide adequate coverage for these particularly valuable items.

Earthquake and Flood Insurance

As you review the exclusion section of your policy you may find some disconcerting exclusions, such as earth movement and water damage. You may obtain some relief from the earth movement exclusion by buying an earthquake rider, which is widely available. However, you may experience more difficulty as you seek to reduce exposure to water damage and flood. Commercial insurance companies have not been able to provide flood insurance profitably since people who live on mountains won't buy it, and those who live in river valleys and lowlands always buy it. As a result, the Federal Government has a federally subsidized program for flood insurance. The federal program offers only limited coverage, as shown in Figure 4–5.

The Federal program provides basic protection and safety, it does not replace elaborate basement recreation rooms. Those of you who are living in lowlands where the coverage is particularly desirable will find, as expected, that your costs will be significant. The Action Letter asks your insurance professional to let you know the cost of both earthquake and flood insurance, and gives him the opportunity to address your needs for that type of coverage.

Figure 4–4
Personal Property Limitations Under Homeowner's Policy

Item	Dollar Limit of Indemnification
1. Money, Bank Notes, Boullion, Coins, and Metals	$ 200
2. Securities, Manuscripts, Stamp Collections and Valuable Papers	1,000
3. Watercraft Including their Trailers, Equipment and Motors	1,000
4. Trailers	1,000
5. Grave Markers	1,000
6. Loss of Jewelry, Watches, Fur, and Precious and Semi-Precious Stones by Theft	1,000
7. Loss of Firearms by Theft	2,000
8. Loss of Silverware, Silverplateware, Goldware, Goldplateware, and Pewter by Theft	2,500
9. Property on the Residence Premises Used for Business Purposes	2,500
10. Property Away from the Resident Premises Used for Business Purposes	250

Residential Worker's Compensation

Another confusing aspect of homeowner's insurance is the requirement in some states, for worker's compensation insurance if you hire domestic help or other occasional workers to do household work for you. You may be liable in these situations whether or not you are aware of the requirement. It is wise to be prepared for the problem. For this reason, in the Action Letter we ask that your insurance professional inform you of any requirements that might be unique to your particular area.

Figure 4–5
Federal Flood Insurance

Basement
Items Covered   *Items Excluded*

Foundation   Furniture
Furnace   Cabinets
Heating Duct Work   Pool Tables
Air Conditioner   Televisions
Water Heater   Stereos
Washer and Dryer   Walls and Ceilings Finished
Floors
Food Freezer
Sump Pump
Electric Service

The Average Policy provides $70,000 in Coverage and Costs $230 per year.

Safety Devices Reduce Homeowner Policy Premium

You have the opportunity to reduce the annual cost of your homeowner's insurance policy using the "control" treatment of risk rather than the "financing" treatment that insurance represents. We suggest that you reduce your exposure to loss by instituting safety procedures and purchasing safety devices. You will be able to reduce the annual cost of your homeowner's policy by purchasing and installing smoke detectors, fire extinguishers, dead-bolt locks and possibly other protective devices. This, too, is included in the Action Letter, both to inform you and to encourage you to adopt such procedures and make such purchases. It also lets your insurance professional know that you have done so.

It is also important for you to inform your insurance professional if you are conducting any business pursuits within your home, so that appropriate business insurance protection may be purchased. Home businesses are growing in popularity and opportunity, and they require appropriate insurance coverage.

Renter/Condominium Dwellers Insurance

You will note on Figure 4–3 that renter's insurance is referred to as an HO-4 policy. It provides broad form coverage for your personal property, and reimbursement for any *loss of use* of your rental property to the extent of 20% of your personal property coverage. Renter's frequently need riders to provide adequate protection by extending and increasing the benefits of the standard HO-4 policy. The standard HO-4 rental policy and HO-6 condominium dwellers policies provide no liability coverage automatically, so renters and condominium dwellers should make special arrangements for a general liability policy (See Chapter Six).

Condominium owners are responsible for the physical repair of everything within the walls of the condominium unit, and therefore should have coverage (HO-6) that will provide indemnification in case of the interior destruction of their unit. Condominium owners also have a responsibility for the common elements of their condominium complex, insurance for which is normally provided by the condominium association. However, it is *your* property and you would be wise to make sure that adequate coverage has been obtained. You may purchase "loss assessment" insurance that will pay up to a stipulated amount for assessments made against you by your association for both common element losses and liability suits filed against your association. You will want to have this cost-effective type of coverage.

Special Situation Homes

Many privately owned free standing homes will not qualify for an HO-1, HO-2, HO-3 or HO-5 policy, either as a result of their location/or their construction. Replacement, either partially or wholly, of these properties would be impractical or impossible. For example, you might have a very old home with irreplaceable, elaborate woodwork and stained glass windows; or an older home in a very remote area that has no market value. It could be an elaborate home, expensive to replace, built in a neighborhood where it would not now be replaced, even if it could be, if it was totally destroyed. Insurance companies have found under circumstances such as these that their risk of such structures being destroyed by fire increases dramatically. As a result, they seek to limit their exposure by providing a special contract for such structures, referred to as an HO-8 policy. The HO-8 policy limits the amount under Coverage A that it will provide for replacement reimbursement for the dwelling. Reimbursement under Coverage A will be provided only for the basic risks listed in the policy, and reimbursement will be on actual cash value only, that is, the replacement cost less depreciation. If you own such a structure, discuss its coverage with your property/casualty insurance professional. Be aware of the limits of your coverage and the extent to which you are self-insuring the dwelling. With this type of structure, control techniques become your primary risk-management tool because financing techniques (i.e., insurance) are limited.

Summary

In reviewing your residence and real estate insurance, make sure that the declarations pages of your policies specifically refer to each piece of real estate that you personally own. If a particular piece of real estate is not listed on any of your policies, you are exposed to losses for which you are personally liable without the assistance of insurance.

There are certain actions that you must take if you do experience a loss. These are listed within the Conditions and Exclusions area of your policy. It is important to comply with these conditions in order to collect any claim you make against your insurer. The steps that you can expect to see within your policy are as follows:

1. Give immediate written notice of the loss.
2. Protect the property from further damage.
3. Separate the damaged property from the undamaged.
4. Furnish an inventory of the damaged property with its costs, values, description of damage, and losses sustained.
5. Provide written proof of loss within 60 days including detailed information about the loss, such as the time of occurrence, origin, your insurable interest, occupancy, other insurance contracts in force, and so on.
6. Exhibit to the insurer the property and books of account.

Follow the steps specifically outlined in your policy. Cooperate fully with the insurer; do things in writing and do them promptly.

FIVE

VEHICLE INSURANCE

The ensuing discussion of vehicle insurance will not be limited to the family automobile only. As we did with real estate, we want to make sure that every vehicle you own is on the inventory page. The inventory for vehicle insurance, appears in Figure 5–1. It should list every licensed vehicle that you own including motorcycles, airplanes, boats, and so on.

More than 39 states have laws that require the registered owners of vehicles to have insurance. Many other states have financial responsibility laws that allow for the revocation of your license and registration unless you can demonstrate your ability to pay any judgments that may result from an accident. Vehicle insurance is a must for vehicle owners.

Who Is Covered?

You, your spouse who is a resident in your same household,

Figure 5–1
Vehicle Insurance Inventory

Company/ Vehicle	Liability Coverage	Medical Payment	Collision Deduct/ Premium	Comp. Deduct/ Premium	Uninsured Motorist Coverage	Policy Number	Annual Premium
1	—	—	—	—	—	—	—
2	—	—	—	—	—	—	—

Total Vehicle Premium: ___

and other family members related by blood, marriage or adoption, including a ward or foster child who is a resident in your household, and who reasonably believe they are entitled to use one of your vehicles, are covered persons. If any of these people should happen to injure a bright, young medical student, to such an extent that the medical student is prevented from practicing medicine for the rest of his life, you could find yourself the object of a judgment that could force you into personal bankruptcy. However, even personal bankruptcy would not relieve you of the obligation of paying the judgment as a result of the injuries to that young student. Such a judgement could follow you the rest of your life. Substantial coverage is essential to your economic health.

Anyone who is going to operate a motor vehicle must be protected to the maximum extent possible against such losses.

The Inventory

Refer to your vehicle policies and fill in the vehicle insurance inventory in Figure 5–1. Record the insurance company and the vehicle(s) covered under that policy. Liability coverage is of primary importance because this is the area in which you have the most to lose. The Action Letter (Figure 5–2) recommends that you increase your liability coverage to the maximum practical limit coordinated with your umbrella or comprehensive personal liability policy. You will find hundreds of examples of automobile accidents and injuries that have resulted in judgments against car owners for one million dollars and more. However, you will not find many insurance companies that will issue an automobile policy with a one million dollar liability section. As a result, we recommend the personal umbrella liability policy or the personal comprehensive liability policy, which we will discuss in more depth in the next chapter.

Figure 5–2
Vehicle Action Letter

Dear _____:

I am evaluating my vehicle insurance, and I would appreciate your assistance.

My specific requests concerning my VEHICLE coverages are as follows:

1. Provide the MAXIMUM available UNINSURED and UN-DERINSURED motorist coverage.

2. Provide the MAXIMUM available MEDICAL payments coverage.

3. Make collision and comprehensive insurance cost-effective by not providing collision coverage on a vehicle whose replacement cost is not cost-effective to insure. I would also like to use cost-effective deductibles. What changes would you recommend to bring my insurance into compliance with these two objectives?

4. Increase my LIABILITY coverage to the MAXIMUM practical limit, keeping in mind that I would like to have it coordinate with my 'personal umbrella policy.'

Please let me know if there are any other provisions, endorsements or riders that should be added to my policy.

Sincerely,

Medical Payments

The medical payments provision that you will find on the declarations page of your automobile policy is the next thing to record on your inventory. This is a special form of accident insurance which provides coverage for medical expenses incurred by insured persons in automobile accidents. The standard limit for most policies is $1,000 per person; however, this limit can be raised by the payment of a small additional premium. Basically, the medical payments provision is designed to pay reasonable expenses incurred for necessary medical and funeral expenses because of bodily injury caused by accident and sustained by a covered person. It usually limits the payment of these expenses to within three years of the date of the accident.

Vehicle insurance, unlike a homeowner's policy, applies to the named insured—you and your family members—who suffer bodily injury caused by an accident while occupying a covered automobile. The coverage will also apply to you and your family members if, while you are pedestrians, you are struck by a motor vehicle designed for use on the public roads or by a trailer of any type. Additionally, people other than the named insured and family members are covered for medical payments while occupying your covered auto.

There are a number of circumstances under which you will not be covered by this provision. You will not be covered for vehicles with less than four wheels, e.g., the three-wheeled all-terrain vehicle. You will not be covered in autos that are used for carrying people or property for a fee, or if you are injured in your employer provided vehicle. Business vehicles need business policies. Additionally, you will not be covered in an auto that you are operating without a reasonable belief that you are entitled to do so.

Your action letter asks for the maximum medical payments coverage available. You will be surprised at the small additional cost it takes to significantly increase this coverage above its $1,000 minimum to an amount that would provide reasonable benefits in the event of an injury.

It could be argued that since most people are covered under some form of individual health insurance, medical payments coverage is redundant. However, there are too many circumstances where you, your family members, or the passengers in your vehicle may be temporarily without medical coverage. For example, your dependent child may be a recent graduate who no longer fits the definition of "dependent and in school" and may, therefore, not be covered under your employer provided group medical insurance. If Murphy's Law prevails, that is when an accident will occur. This is another area where the general rule, "don't risk a lot for a little," is applicable.

Collision Coverage

The next section in your vehicle insurance inventory concerns collision and comprehensive coverages. Record your deductible on these two coverages alongside the premium, since deductibles are usually effective in controlling premium costs in this area. By doing so you and your insurance agent will be able to compare alternate deductibles and the associated costs with the most cost-effective combination.

Collision coverage is to indemnify you for losses caused by the upset of your covered auto or its collision with another object. This coverage is provided regardless of who is at fault in the accident and will apply when you cannot recover damages from another party whose negligence was the cause of your loss. This provision makes sure that you can get your vehicle back in operation as quickly as possible. Your insurance company may make a claim against the negligent party's insurance company and seek reimbursement from that company.

Comprehensive Coverage

If you sustain a loss other than as a result of the upset of your vehicle or its collision with another object, you will be reimbursed under the comprehensive section of your policy.

You would make a claim under the comprehensive section of your policy for such occurrences as broken glass, losses caused by missiles or flying objects, fire, theft, larceny, explosion, earthquake, windstorm, hail, water, flood, malicious mischief or vandalism, a riot or civil commotion, or contact with a bird or animal.

Since the deductible on your comprehensive coverage is often lower than the deductible on your collision coverage you normally would prefer to make a claim under your comprehensive coverage.

There are, however, a number of exclusions under comprehensive coverage that you should be aware of, such as the theft or destruction of citizens band radio equipment and sound and video equipment within your vehicle. If you have this type of valuable equipment, you will want to request additional riders to make sure that it is covered.

The amount that you can expect your insurer to pay for physical damage to your vehicle will be either the actual cash value of the damaged or stolen property, meaning its replacement value less an allowance for depreciation, or the amount required to repair or replace the property, preferably the latter.

Uninsured/Underinsured Motorist Coverage

In spite of mandatory insurance in some 39 states and financial responsibility regulations in practically all states that insist that people have either adequate insurance or adequate resources to satisfy judgments against them before driving an automobile, people still drive motor vehicles without insurance. For example, in Cook County, Illinois, which includes the city of Chicago, it has been reported that half of the drivers on the road do not have insurance. In California, it is estimated that two million of the eleven million vehicles registered in that state are uninsured. It is typically people without resources that drive motor vehicles without insurance.

If you were to have an accident in either the Chicago area or California under those circumstances, the odds are pretty high that the person who hits you will be one of those people without insurance and without resources. How, then, and from whom are you going to be indemnified for your losses? Look at your inventory of vehicle insurance in Figure 5–1. Have you filled in the section under uninsured/underinsured motorist coverage? If you have recorded $15,000 /$30,000, which is the amount that we see much too often, you are severely underinsured.

How will you be sufficiently covered with a limit of $15,000 per person, and $30,000 per accident, as the maximum that your insurance company will reimburse you? Underinsured motorist coverage is to protect you, not others. The Action Letter requests the maximum uninsured/underinsured motorist coverage. The declarations page in your policy will state how much you are paying for that coverage at the present time. You can probably increase the reimbursement to $100,000/$300,000 for an insignificant increase in premium.

The increase in the premium applies to coverage that you are purchasing for you, your family members and any other person occupying your insured automobile. In fact, it also applies to you and your family members if you are injured as pedestrians or while on a bicycle. Again—don't risk a lot for a little.

The underinsured provision in your coverage exists because some people have insurance with limits that are too low to protect you adequately. If you or your family sustain losses exceeding the other driver's coverage, you may find yourself claiming under your own coverage.

No Fault

No fault insurance has received a great deal of attention in the press. Indeed, you might be a resident of a state that requires no fault coverage to some degree. The personal auto policies issued in such states will be in compliance with the state regulations. Your policy should be flexible in its provisions, since you may not be involved in an accident in your own state.

The concept of no fault insurance is to save money by not having to go through the process of determining who is at fault. The conventional means of indemnification, which necessitates determining who is at fault and who pays, takes time and also may involve substantial legal fees. No fault in its pure form means that there is no relevance to who caused the accident that resulted in bodily injury. The insured party suffering the loss would seek recovery for medical expenses, loss of income and other expenses from his or her own insurer, and there would be no claim for general damages or suffering. This pure form of no fault coverage has not been a very popular concept. No one wishes to give up the right to sue people who cause them general damage and suffering.

Modified no fault, however, provides limited immunity from the requirement to establish blame in the event of an automobile accident. Under modified no fault, a certain amount of expense will be indemnified under first party coverage; that is your own policy will reimburse you regardless of fault. Beyond that limited amount, liability would be determined and you would seek recovery from the party at fault. Treatment of claims for pain and suffering vary from state to state under the modified plans. The Catch-22 in no fault coverage is that although we all would like to eliminate the expense of lawyers and the legal process necessary to obtain just compensation, the idea that a negligent driver does not have personal responsibility is repugnant to most of us.

Another pseudo form of no fault insurance is expanded first party coverage. This type of coverage expedites the claim for injuries after an accident, allowing the individual to make claims against his own insurance company. However, the insurance company may then sue the negligent driver's insurance company to recover the amount paid to its insured who was not at fault. This is not really no fault coverage since the negligent driver is not freed of responsibility.

Who Is Insured?

Your personal auto policy covers you, or any family member while using any auto or trailer. "You," in this case, refers to the named insured listed on the declarations page of the insurance policy and his or her spouse if a resident in the same household. "Family member" refers to a person related to the named insured by blood, marriage or adoption, including a ward or foster child who is a resident of the named insured's household. The term "resident" has a special legal connotation and may extend beyond the confines of the insured's dwelling. A son or daughter away at school or in the military may still be considered a resident of the household as long as the household is considered "home" and there is an intent to return to the household. Although the covered person definition does not make reference to a requirement of permission, the policy normally will exclude coverage of anyone operating a vehicle without a reasonable belief that he or she is entitled to do so. Also note that the coverage applies to the operation of both the covered vehicle and non-owned (borrowed or rented) vehicles.

In certain situations, suit for liability may be placed against the driver of a vehicle and, if that driver is on company business, the driver's employer. If that employee was driving a vehicle owned by someone else, that employee would be covered as an insured under his own policy while driving the non-owned vehicle and coverage may be extended to that driver's employer. However, if you are routinely driving for your employer both your own and your employers property/casualty agent should be made aware of the situation to assure proper coverage is in force.

In order to be eligible for the packaged personal automobile policy, a vehicle must be owned by an individual or by a husband and wife "who are residents of the same household." It is entirely possible that a husband and wife may not be legal residents of the same household, and therefore their qualification for a personal auto policy for a jointly owned vehicle may terminate. In this case, alternative coverage should be sought immediately.

Which Vehicles Are Covered?

Any vehicle that is shown on the declarations page is covered. Check your inventory page; are all vehicles that you own listed on that page, and are they included in the declarations pages as covered vehicles under appropriate policies?

In addition to the vehicles indicated on the declarations page, you will be insured for any vehicle for which you acquire ownership during the policy period, providing you ask the insurance company to insure it within 30 days of becoming the owner. This will apply to private passenger cars, and, as long as they are not used in business, pick-ups, panel trucks and vans. Also covered is any trailer that you might own and any non-owned auto or trailer being used as a temporary substitute for any vehicle described above which is out of normal use because of breakdown, repair, service, loss or destruction.

Rental Cars

Anytime you rent an automobile, you are encouraged to purchase a collision damage waiver to eliminate your liability for the deductible or any uninsured losses to which the rental car agency is exposed. The typical charge of nine dollars per day totals up to $3,285 per year, which is a rather significant premium to have to pay for a potential loss of $500 to $3,000. In most cases, your personal auto policy or family auto policy will provide coverage to indemnify you for the payment of any of these deductibles. However, problems can occur when you return to the rental agency on a Sunday night with a damaged vehicle and have difficulty proving that you do have coverage to pay the bill. The rental agency could demand immediate damage payment. In order to avoid these problems and indeed in response to these problems, credit card agencies have included in their package of benefits automatic coverage stipulating that if you rent a car using their credit card, they assume this liability. In most cases, the rental car agencies have accepted this type of coverage and have not hassled renters for immediate payments. This appears to be a very satisfactory solution to the problem, and furthermore you are able to save the nine dollars per day charged for the damage waiver. Check with your credit card company for the availability of this benefit.

Other Vehicles

You will want to make sure that all motorcycles, mopeds, all-terrain vehicles, snowmobiles and other miscellaneous vehicles that you own are covered by your policy or an endorsement on your policy referred to as a "miscellaneous vehicle endorsement." There is no coverage under the endorsement for rented or borrowed vehicles of this type. Caution is advised whenever you rent a recreational vehicle. Read the waivers you are asked to sign and consider the risks that you may be taking. For instance, don't sign for your neighbor's children—their own parents should be there to do it for them.

If you have business vehicles, you will find that each is unique and needs its own special insurance. Consult your property casualty insurance professional.

Duties After an Accident or Loss

An automobile accident is normally a traumatic experience, and most of us do not think clearly when involved in one. Therefore, it is wise to know what you have to do in the event of an accident.

1. Cooperate with the insurer in the investigation, defense or settlement
2. Promptly send the insurer copies of any notices or legal papers received in connection with a loss
3. Submit to physical examinations by physicians selected by the insurer as often as the insurer reasonably requires. The insurer pays the cost of the examination
4. Authorize the insurer to obtain medical reports and other pertinent records

5. Submit proof of loss when required by the insurer

Whenver the police are involved, it is essential to acquire a copy of their reports. This is particularly important when seeking coverage under uninsured motorist coverage. Prompt notification of the police in the event of a hit-and-run situation is essential.

In the case of physical damage to your vehicle, you are also obligated to take reasonable steps after your loss to protect the auto and equipment from further loss. The insurer will pay expenses incurred by you in providing this protection. The police must be notified in the event a vehicle is stolen and you must allow the insurance company to inspect and appraise the damaged vehicle before you repair it or dispose of it.

Summary

The basic premise of this chapter is that you are going to buy vehicle insurance. You are not going to drive without it. You may have gotten the feeling that the advice on the previous pages was given without an awareness of how expensive vehicle insurance can be. We do advise that you maximize liability (coordinated with your umbrella coverage), medical payments and uninsured/underinsured motorist coverage, because mediocre insurance coverage is not cost-effective. The additional premium to go from mediocre coverage, that fails you when you need it, to quality coverage, that protects you when it is supposed to, represents some of the most important money you will ever spend on insurance. All vehicle insurance is costly, but to upgrade to the best coverage is really not that much more expensive and represents a wise purchase—one that you will appreciate at claim time.

One of the best ways to save money on insurance is to carefully select the vehicles you drive. The make and model of your vehicle dictates the cost of your policy. Know what insurance is going to cost you before you buy a vehicle. If insurance costs influence your choice, chances are you'll be saving more than just the premiums. You'll be saving all the other costs associated with high insurance cost such as high purchase price, high repair bills, low gas mileage, and so on.

SIX

LIABILITY INSURANCE

We all face the risk that our behavior could result in injury to another person or damage to someone's property. We are responsible for the results of our behavior. What is unique about liability risk is that it has no maximum predictable limit. If you've read or heard about large liability suits, you've probably thought about what would happen if *you* were the subject of such a suit. If a judgment was won against you, the claimant could take everything you own in addition to whatever insurance you might have. Neither you, your spouse, nor your family members can be expected to behave as reasonable and prudent individuals at all times. We will all, at times, be negligent. If, as a result of one instance of negligence, someone else is subject to a loss as a result of your negligent act, you can expect to be sued and you can expect that the courts will hold in favor of the claimant. To be negligent doesn't mean that you are a bad person; it merely means that you failed to exercise the proper degree of care required under a certain set of circumstances. You made a mistake and mistakes are costly.

In your comprehensive personal liability/umbrella liability inventory shown in Figure 6–1, we first determine who is insured under your umbrella policy and what company is providing the coverage. If you do not have a liability policy, sign and send the Action Letter so that your property casualty insurance professional can give you a quote on a personal liability policy and let you know what is required to put it in force as soon as possible. The letter inquires about the cost of one million dollars of coverage, and then asks the agent to give you the cost of the maximum amount of coverage that you could purchase.

Our minimum recommendation will be a one million dollar policy. We would increase that recommendation based upon what is available to you, your lifestyle and public profile, and what your property and casualty professional recommends. The higher your standard of living, the more you have to lose. The higher your profile, the more the public expects of you, and the more people will react negatively as a result of you or your family's personal negligence that results in damage to another. The more they expect of you, the more they will sue you for. Don't risk a lot for a little—maximize this coverage!

Once negligence has been determined, there must be actual damage or loss as a result of the negligence. In most cases this is measured by the actual monetary loss suffered by the injured party. When one suffers a bodily injury as a result of negligence of another, the injured party may sue for compensatory payments and for *specific* damages such as medical expenses and loss of income. These are relatively easy to measure. In addition to these specific damages, the injured party may also ask for *general damages* to compensate for the intangible losses resulting from pain and suffering, disfigurement, mental anguish and loss of consortium. The monetary value of these losses is more subjective. *Punitive damages*, the third form of damages that may be assessed against the negligent parties, are a form of punishment. An injury to a

Figure 6-1
Comprehensive Personal Liability Insurance

Insured/ Company	Liability Maximum	Policy Type	Deductible	Special Features	Remarks	Policy Number	Annual Premium
1	—	—	—	—	—	—	—
2	—	—	—	—	—	—	—

TOTAL LIABILITY PREMIUM: ____

party which results from gross negligence or willful intent is likely to result in sustainable claims for all three types: specific damages, general damages and punitive damages.

In most cases, the burden of proof of negligence is on the injured party. However, if you break the law and cause an injury, it may be referred to as "negligence per se." The injured party in this case might not have to prove negligence. The fact that you broke the law may be sufficient to establish negligence. In other cases, there is absolute liability. Such liability may be imposed simply because an accident happens. Liability is imposed regardless of whether one can actually be determined to be at fault.

The bottom line is that we all need substantial liability insurance and we all need to know when such insurance will not protect us.

When Insurance Won't Help!

Liability insurance coverage is not likely to assist us if our behavior which is deemed to be negligent occurred while we were breaking the law—committing a criminal or a public wrong. We cannot expect insurance companies to come to our aid if we commit intentional acts to harm others. Nor will it cover any bodily injury or property damage arising out of a business pursuit of any insured. Business pursuit liability insurance needs immediate, proper handling by a qualified property casualty insurance agent.

Comprehensive Personal Liability Insurance Policy

Comprehensive personal liability coverage can be acquired by purchasing a separate comprehensive liability policy or, at times, by purchasing a rider on your individual homeowner policy. You should consult with your property casualty insurance professional to find out which is more appropriate under your personal circumstances.

Under this type of policy, the company will promise to pay, up to the limits of liability set in the policy, all payments that become the insured's legal obligation because of bodily injury or property damage falling within the scope of the coverage provided by the policy. In addition, it will pay the legal expenses and attorney's fees for the insurance company's chosen counsel. The insurance company has the right to settle a claim or suit against you that it decides is appropriate. In addition to the expenses, the contract will pay the interest on judgments plus certain other legal costs.

The insureds under your comprehensive liability policy are you, your relatives who are residents of your household and any other person under age 21 who is in the care of a resident of the household.

The policy will pay all medical expenses, including funeral expenses, incurred by persons who are injured while on the premises with the permission of any insured, or injured away from the premises if injury results from activity of an insured or member of the insured's family. In addition to the claim costs, the policy will also pay for the first-aid expenses incurred by the insured, related to any bodily injury covered under the policy. The policy may even pay some minor amount, usually up to five hundred dollars, for damage to the property of others for which there is no legal obligation on the part of the insured, but which the insured might feel a moral obligation to pay.

Condominium/Common Property Owners

If you own a condominium, your condominium association could be sued as a result of an injury occurring to someone on the condominium common property; in turn, the condominium association may have to assess you in order to obtain funds to pay that judgment. Your comprehensive personal liability policy would provide coverage up to one thousand dollars to pay those assessments. If you feel one thousand dollars is inadequate, you may request an endorsement purchasing additional coverage.

A comprehensive personal liability policy is particularly appropriate for people who do not own their own home or automobile and thus do not have liability protection under their homeowner's or auto policies. Comprehensive personal liability policies do not assume any underlying coverage. The coverage also is appropriate for renters and condominium owners. An Action Letter requesting liability insurance is provided in Figure 6–2.

Umbrella Liability Policy

The personal umbrella liability policy expands the liability coverages home and auto owners normally have within their homeowner's and auto policies. It exists because we all may be subject to liability claims of catastrophic proportions. The umbrella liability policy was originally developed for business purposes and, at one time, was exclusively underwritten by Lloyds of London. It is a broad form of liability coverage covering both general liability and automobile liability, purchased in addition to the separate liability protection provided by the typical auto and homeowner's policies.

In order to qualify for the umbrella liability policy, you will be required to purchase certain underlying liability protection within your homeowner's and/or automobile policies. Each insurance company has its own customary practices regarding the underlying coverage required before they will write an umbrella policy. The objective is to have the umbrella policy written as excess coverage, over the limits of the required basic contracts, with a high limit of liability ranging from one to ten million dollars.

The umbrella policy serves two separate functions. It expands your basic coverage and thus fulfills its first function of "excess coverage," since it will pay in addition to the basic coverage if the basic coverage proves insufficient to pay the claim. For example, if you have $500,000 of coverage under your basic policy and a $1 million umbrella policy, your total coverage for any one liability claim would be $1.5 million.

The second function of your umbrella liability is to establish broader coverage than that provided under the basic contracts. The property casualty Action Letter specifically asks

Figure 6–2
Comprehensive/Umbrella Liability Action Letter

Dear _____ :

I would appreciate it if you would give me a quote on a comprehensive personal liability policy and let me know what is required to put it in force as soon as possible.

Will this coverage increase my existing vehicle/real estate liability coverages? Will it also supplement them by providing protection against certain liability exposures not covered under those policies such as personal injury, invasion of privacy, and liability for most non-owned property in my care, custody or control?

What would be the cost for $1,000,000 in coverage? $ _____

What would be the maximum I could purchase? _____
Cost? _____

I would appreciate any further recommendations that you can make to help me accomplish my objective of being adequately insured for all situations involving potentially severe losses.

Please call me if you have any questions. I look forward to receiving your proposals in the mail so that I may review them with my advisor.

Sincerely,

Enclosure(s): Declarations pages from current real estate, vehicle and liability policies.

your insurance professional to explain how the proposed umbrella policy will work. Will it extend or increase the existing coverage? Will it supplement your existing coverage by providing protection against certain liability exposures that are not covered under your underlying policies? Answers to these specific questions are necessary since umbrella polices are not as standardized as auto and homeowner's policies. It is essential that you ask for an explanation of the specific coverages under your policy.

You want your umbrella liability policy to expand your protection in the areas of slander, defamation of character, invasion of privacy and damages caused by use of non-owned property in your care, custody and control. An example of the latter is a situation in which you had borrowed equipment from a neighbor—such as a lawnmower or snowblower—and, while it was in your care, custody and control, a neighbor's child was hurt with the machine. You would be liable for that injury, subject to suit, and if a judgment were awarded against you, your homeowner's policy would probably not provide coverage, whereas your umbrella liability policy should provide the protection.

If you are in the public eye, quoted in the public press or are simply outspoken, you may be interested in the coverage provided for libel, slander and invasion of privacy. Libel is defamation of character; slander is spoken defamation of character. Invasion of privacy may be claimed by one who feels that his peace of mind has been invaded. People have a right to privacy in personal matters and feel that they should not be commented upon or scrutinized in public without their consent. Additionally, if you are exposed to claims of plagiarism or violation of copyright laws, your comprehensive personal liability or umbrella liability policy could provide protection. It is unlikely that protection would be offered under your homeowner's or auto policy.

One Agent/One Company

Ideally, you will find one capable and competent insurance professional to fill your residence, automobile and liability insurance needs. It is also preferable to have all three policies with one insurance company. The advantage of one agent and one insurance company is that the agent should take a greater interest in your affairs as a result of having all your business. He should also feel a great responsibility for caring for you since he knows he is the only one on whom you rely.

Furthermore, having all of your coverages with one insurance company eliminates the question of which insurance company should pay which claim. Since only one insurance company holds all three policies, that insurance company alone is liable, no matter which of your policies happens to pay the claim. In most cases, a discount is offered to package all three of these coverages together with one insurance company.

In Figure 6–3, we have reconstructed all three sections of your property/casualty insurance Action Letter—real estate, vehicle and liability. Adjust the letter to your needs, sign it and send it to your selected property casualty insurance professional. When you ask your agent in writing to do something for you and to implement a coverage, it creates a responsibility for that agent. If, for some reason, one of your written requests is inadvertently not implemented and, as a result, you are exposed to an uninsured loss, then a photocopy of your written request for coverage may be very valuable to you in your claim against the agent's errors and omissions insurance.

Summary

In Chapter Four we discussed residence and real estate insurance; in Chapter Five we discussed automobile and vehicle insurance; and in this chapter we discussed your liability coverage. All three of these coverages are referred to as property casualty coverages. Consult your property casualty insurance professional for information, advice and implementation of these policies. Having read these three chapters, you can appreciate that these coverages are very detailed and are subject to constant change. You can also see that errors made

Figure 6–3
Combined Vehicle, Real Estate and Liability Action Letter

Dear _____ :

I am evaluating my property casualty insurance, and I would appreciate your assistance.

My specific desires concerning my *vehicle* coverages are as follows:

1. Provide the *maximum* availble *uninsured* and *undersigned* motorist coverage.

2. Provide the *maximum* available *medical* payments coverage.

3. Make collision and comprehensive insurance cost-effective by not providing collision coverage on a vehicle whose replacement cost it is not cost effective to insure. I would also like to use cost-effective deductibles. What changes would you recommend to bring my insurance into compliance with these two objectives?

4. Increase my *liability* coverage to the *maximum* practical limit, keeping in mind that I would like to have it coordinate with my 'personal umbrella policy.'

REAL ESTATE INSURANCE:

Please provide me with a quote on my Residence/Real Estate insurance coverage based on the following parameters:

1. Maintain my *liability* at the maximum amount available or the amount that would best coordinate with a personal umbrella liability policy.

2. Make sure that the coverage is of the most *comprehensive all-risk* variety. I would like the most comprehensive HO form including coverage for personal property losses and indirect losses resulting from the loss of use of personal property.

3. Loss payments are to be made on a *"replacement cost"* basis rather than an "actual cash value" depreciated value basis for all coverages including personal property.

4. Please let me know if there are any discounts available for the following:

	I HAVE	DO NOT HAVE
Smoke Detectors	_____	_____
Fire Extinguishers	_____	_____

Deadbolt Locks   _____   _____
Other Protective
Devices   _____   _____

5. Do I require any special coverages for our household domestic help and/or other occasional workers we hire for household work?

6. Please recommend *cost-effective* deductibles.

7. Please maximize *guest medical.*

8. Please let me know the cost of *earthquake* and/or *flood* coverage and your recommendations regarding my need for such coverage.

9. Special items of value that should be included on a personal property rider are as follows:

ITEM	VALUE	APPRAISAL METHOD/DATE
_____	_____	_____
_____	_____	_____
_____	_____	_____
_____	_____	_____

10. Do you recommend any *business pursuits endorsements?*

COMPREHENSIVE PERSONAL LIABILITY (UMBRELLA) POLICY:

I would appreciate it if you would give me a quote on a comprehensive personal liability policy.

Will this coverage increase my existing vehicle/real estate liability coverages? Will it also supplement them by providing protection against certain liability exposures not covered under those policies such as personal injury, invasion of privacy, and liability for most non-owned property in my care, custody or control?

What would be the cost for $1,000,000 in coverage? $ _____

What would be the maximum I could purchase? _____ Cost? _____

I would appreciate any further recommendations that you can make to help me accomplish my objective of being adequately insured for all situations involving potentially severe losses.

Sincerely,

Enclosure(s): Copies of current declarations pages from existing real estate, vehicle and liability policies.

in your policies can expose you to significant losses. We suggest that you buy your property casualty policies from *one* competent professional and from *one* company, if possible. The people from whom you purchase your policy will earn a commission as a result of selling to you. Even sales representatives from "no load" or "low load" insurance organizations such as United Services Automobile Association which sells insurance via telephone, are compensated. They earn a salary to serve you and they deserve to earn it. The most highly qualified professional to assist you in the area of property casualty insurance is the Chartered Property and Casualty Underwriter, CPCU. The more complex and important your property casualty needs, the more important it is that you find a properly trained and licensed agent willing and capable to serve your needs.

SEVEN

LIFE INSURANCE

Life Insurance n.:

insurance providing for payment of a single stipulated sum to a designated beneficiary upon the death of the insured.

Webster's Third International Dictionary

A more pragmatic definition of life insurance may be that it is "insurance company money to be received by a beneficiary upon the death of the insured." (*The Life Insurance Investment Advisor*, Baldwin and Droms, Probus, 1988.)

Why Have Life Insurance?

The answer to the question, "Do I need any life insurance?," depends on your answers to two more questions. The first is, "In the event of my death, will anyone experience an economic loss?" If the answer to that question is yes, someone will experience an economic loss, then you are ready for the second question: "Do you care?" If you do not, then you have

111

determined that you do not need life insurance. However, if you do care, then you do need life insurance.

Life insurance guarantees that the person who will take an economic loss in the event of your death will be indemnified for that loss. Replacing human life value is the primary purpose of life insurance, and that is what is totally unique about this product. No other contract or property that you can buy will do what a life insurance contract will do for your beneficiaries.

Determining the amount of life insurance you want for your beneficiary in a family situation is a very personal decision. This book, and your life insurance advisor, can assist you in determining your needs, but the final decision will be a value judgment of your own.

The Inventory

The life insurance inventory shown in Figure 7–1 is our first effort to get your current life insurance policies up-to-date. Fill in the name of the family member whose life insurance is being inventoried then inventory the policies on the life of that individual, recording first the insurance company providing the coverage and second, the type of policy. If you have difficulty determining the type of your policy, look at the bottom of the front page of the contract at the small print. Usually you will find a short statement of exactly what type of policy it is, such as whole life, term insurance, universal life, variable life, or a universal variable type of policy. Next record the policy number and the register date (date the policy went into effect) indicated within the policy. Record the death benefit followed by the full asset value of the policy. The asset value of the policy is the amount that the insurance company would pay you for that policy if you cashed it in for its cash surrender value. If you have borrowed against the policy, record the amount of the policy loan in the next column. If your policy is other than term insurance, and therefore does have an increase in cash value each year, record the latest annual increase in cash value in the next column. Next,

Figure 7-1
Life Insurance Inventory

Insured/ Company	Type of Policy	Policy Number	Register Date	Death Benefit	Asset Value	Policy Loan	Annual Cash Value Increase	Annual Premium	Annual Dividend
Name/									
1									
2									
TOTALS				—	—	—	—	—	—

Total Asset Value _____ —

Total Policy Loans _____ —

Total Annual Cash Value Increase _____ —

Total Premium _____ —

Total Annual Dividends _____ —

BENEFICIARIES OF POLICIES

Primary Beneficiary	Secondary Beneficiary	Policy Features	Loan Rate
1			
2			

record the annual premium and the annual dividend that you may be receiving from the contract. Record the *gross* annual premium, not the annual premium reduced by the dividend. In the section at the lower part of your inventory page beside the number 1, record the primary beneficiary for policy number 1, the secondary beneficiary, and the policy features such as waiver of premium, accidental death benefit, the existence of any surrender charges or contingent withdrawal charges, and so on. Do this for each policy on your life. Carefully check those beneficiary provisions—you would be surprised how often they turn out to be inappropiate. Finally, record the interest rate that the insurance company would charge if you should take a policy loan.

Once you have completed the inventory, total up your present life insurance. If you are in doubt about the beneficiary provision on your existing life insurance, use Figure 7–2, the Request for Policy Information form. This form provides a means of asking your insurance company for information regarding your policies. It also provides a place to ask for forms such as a change of beneficiary or change of owner forms. Complete and send in new beneficiary forms if there is any doubt about the accuracy of your present beneficiary designation.

Completing this inventory will help you answer the questions that we will be asking in the coming pages. Has the insurance that you purchased in the past been right for you? Is there any way that you can improve your current life insurance? Do you have enough for your present/future circumstances? Do you have the right kind of life insurance in light of your present and future needs?

Determining Your Life Insurance Requirements

Now that you have inventoried your policies and made the logical corrections to have them best serve your family, it is time to determine their sufficiency. How much life insurance do you need based upon *your* requirements? We will start with an objective form that will assist you in considering

Figure 7–2

REQUEST FOR POLICY INFORMATION

TO: _____   Date _____
  (Company Name)

_____ Re: _____
  (Address)   (Insured)

_____ Policy No.: _____

Please forward the following information on the above Policy for the items below:

(1) Kind of policy _____
  Is accidental death included? _____ Disability premium waiver? _____
(2) Register date _____ Age at issue _____
(3) Face amount _____
(4) Commuted value of any family income type provision or decreasing term as of current date _____ Expiry date _____
(5) Owner of policy _____
(6) Succesive or contingent owner _____
(7) Beneficiary: Primary _____ Secondary _____
(8) How settled? (If other than single sum please indicate withdrawal rights, power of appointment, and terms of simultaneous death provision) _____
(9) Assignments _____
(10) Summarize any physical or occupational ratings _____
(11) Amount of premium _____ Payable _____
(12) Premium paid to _____
(13) Current dividend election _____
(14) Amount of current year's dividend _____
(15) Supplemmental one-year term insurance now in force through use of dividends _____
(16) Cumulative amount of dividends now credited to policy:
   Paid-up additional insurance _____
   Cash value of additional insurance _____
   Accumulations at interest _____
(17) Please send form for new dividend election, policy loans and change of beneficiary _____
(18) Outstanding loans _____
(19) Guaranteed cash value, as of, previous year, current year, next year and age 65. _____
(20) Provide policy cost basis _____
(21) Provide gain/loss position as of this time _____

Please send the requested information
and/or necessary forms to:

     X _____
       Policyowner Signature

specific needs, and conclude with a subjective value judgment that you will apply to the information on the objective form.

Figure 7–3 is a checklist for determining how much insurance would be needed for the immediate expenses that will be incurred in the event of your death and the cash funds you may wish to provide for your family. As we describe each item, we will give you some basic rules of thumb which you may then adjust to your own personal circumstances.

Probate and Administration Expenses

When you die, you will undoubtedly own property that will have to pass to the ownership of others. The type of property that we are concerned with in the probate process is not jointly held property, beneficiary property or living trust property On that property you have already designated who should be the succeeding owner at your death via a beneficiary provision, a joint ownership arrangement or a living trust provision. Property and assets owned in those three ways will pass to those whom you have properly and rightfully designated in accordance with the instructions that you have left within those documents. There will be no need for those assets to pass through the probate process.

The probate process is concerned with those assets that you own in your individual name only. Your will provides the only instructions available to determine the proper disposition of that property at your death. Some readers may conclude that they have no probate property—everything they own is either in joint tenancy with the right of survivorship or controlled by a beneficiary provision or a living trust—and therefore they do not require a will. This assumption is in error! All of us own some personal effects. These personal effects can have substantial value. It would be irresponsible, expensive and a disservice to your beneficiaries to leave the disposition of these assets up to the probate court and the state laws. In addition, you cannot really know the size of your probate estate, that is, what you will own in your own name at death. If your death was caused by an accident and

Figure 7–3
Life Insurance Needs Analyzer
Funds Required for Cash Expenses & Sinking Funds

1. Probate and Administration Expenses:
   a. 5% of Probate Property   _____
   b. 2% of Non-Probate   _____
   c. ?% for Complexity   _____
2. Funeral Expenses   _____
3. Special Obligations   _____
   Pledges   _____
   Contracts   _____
   Divorce   _____
   Business   _____
4. Debts/Insurance Loans/Current Bills   _____
5. Income Tax Liabilities:
   a. Year of Death Return   _____
   b. Retirement Plan Pay Out   _____
   c. IRA/KEOGH/TSA Pay Outs   _____
   d. Deferred Annuity Pay Outs   _____
   e. Tax Shelter - Liability Exceeds:
      1. Basis   _____
      2. Fair Market Value   _____
6. Federal Estate Taxes   _____
7. State Inheritance Taxes   _____
8. Education Fund
   (Calculated or Today's Cost Estimate)   _____
9 Mortage(s)   _____
10. Extra Fund for Error/
    Family Emergency Fund

Funds Required For Cash Expenses & Sinking Funds: _____

your estate placed a suit against a negligent party, a judgement could be won in favor of your estate which would increase its value beyond what you ever contemplated during life. Another "good news, bad news" scenario that would substantially inflate the value of your estate would be that you won a lottery, the excitement caused a heart attack, and you died. Who should receive your lottery winnings? Either you have stated your wishes in your will or the probate law of your state will assume control.

In short, you need a will. You also need a properly qualified and licensed attorney to assist you in drafting that will. Forget the do-it-yourself forms—that comes under the category of risking a lot for a little. Figure 7–4 paraphrases what could happen to your family and your assets if your probate estate has to be distributed under the provisions of the probate code of your state of residence. It is adapted from the "no will" will that appeared in a publication of the Chicago Title and Trust Company of Chicago, Illinois, many years ago. It is intended to emphasize the importance of having a will drafted. By all means, do not do your loved ones the disservice of dying without a will.

The probate process itself is the court's way of making sure that your assets go to the right people. The courts do this by confirming that your will is a properly prepared and executed legal document that clearly expresses your wishes and that your beneficiaries and creditors are treated fairly. Since this entails legal fees, court costs and bonds, and so on, it can be very expensive. It is also very public since all potential beneficiaries and creditors need to be informed so that they can present their claims to the court. It can also cause a great deal of delay since it can take a long time to settle conflicting claims. For these reasons, we recommend that you assume that probate costs will run about 5% of the value of the property that will have to pass through your probate estate on its way to your beneficiaries—see Figure 7–3. The expenses connected with your non-probate property, such as joint tenancy and beneficiary property can be estimated at approximately 2% since they will pass without delay or publicity. As regards "complexity," if your estate is difficult to value and/or could create disputes among creditors and/or beneficiaries at your death, the expenses and delays can be expected to increase exponentially. If you do not have a will, you probably should allow for such expenses here. In Figure 7–3, the entry 1.c. "? for Complexity" will depend on the amount of attention given to planning your estate. The less you prepare prior to death, the more it will cost your survivors.

Figure 7–4

YOUR "NO WILL" WILL
Written For You By Your State of Residence

I hereby do make, publish and declare this to be my Last Will and Testament by failing to have a Will of my own choice prepared.

FIRST ARTICLE

I give my wife only one-half of my possessions, and I give my child or children the remaining one-half. If my wife is not living, all goes to the children, (or their children if they are not living), equally. If I have no spouse or no children, then all I have is to go to my parents, double share if only one is living, and to my brothers and sisters equally, or to the children of any deceased brothers and sisters.

I appoint my wife as guardian of my children, but as a safeguard, I require that she report to the Probate Court each year and render an accounting of how, why and where she spent the money necessary for the proper care of my children.

As a further safeguard, I direct my wife to produce to the Probate Court a Performance Bond to guarantee that she exercises proper judgement in the handling, investing and spending of the children's money.

As a final safeguard, my children shall have the right to demand and receive a complete accounting from their mother of all of her financial actions with their money as soon as they reach legal age.

When my children reach age eighteen, they shall have full rights to withdraw and spend their share of my estate. No one shall have any right to question my children's actions on how they decide to spend their respective shares.

SECOND ARTICLE

Should my wife remarry, her second husband shall be entitled to his marital share of everything my wife possesses.

Should my children need some of this share for their support, the second husband shall not be bound to spend any part of his share on my children's behalf.

The second husband shall have sole right to decide who is to get his share, even to the exclusion of my children.

THIRD ARTICLE

Should my wife predecease me or die while any of my children are minors, I do not wish to exercise my right to nominate the guardian of my children.

Rather than nominating a guardian of my preference, I direct my relatives and friends to get together and select a guardian by mutual agreement.

In the event that they fail to agree on a guardian, I direct the Probate Court to make the selection. If the court wishes, it may appoint a stranger acceptable to it.

FOURTH ARTICLE

Under existing tax law, there are certain legitimate avenues open to me to lower death taxes. Since I prefer to have my money used for governmental purposes rather than for the benefit of my family, I direct that no effort be made to lower taxes.

NO SIGNATURE REQUIRED

If reading these words makes you nervous, your estate planning team comprised of your Certified Public Accountant (CPA), attorney, a competent, professional life insurance salesperson and your trust officer can help a great deal in alleviating potential problems. If you are concerned about incurring legal fees, visit first with the trust officer and a professional life insurance salesperson. This is not to say that buying life insurance automatically solves these problems, but since many estate problems can be solved utilizing life insurance, the professional agent is perfectly willing to take the time to educate you, without charge, in hopes of earning a sale. Many of these problems are solved utilizing living trusts, and thus the trust officer is willing to take the time to educate you, with the hope that he will earn your future trust business. Each, without charge, will help you determine what work will be required of your attorney. In this way, the attorney does not have to bill you for those education hours—you get them free.

Now that you know where the probate and administrative expense estimates come from, record the numbers that you would expect for your own personal estate.

Funeral Expenses

Throughout this book we have given you recommendations that you can adjust to your own circumstances. For example, we now recommend that you record $5,000 for funeral expenses. Some of you will think this sum is ridiculously low; others inordinately high. The proper amount will, in the end, be determined by whatever arrangements you personally find suitable and tasteful.

Special Obligations

In this section, record any pledges you have made to charity that you wish to see completed; any contractual obligations that you might have; any requirements binding you under divorce decrees; and also any business obligations that you wish to see completed. Do you have any children or other relatives who have special needs that you wish to provide for? If so, value those needs and enter the amounts here.

Debts, Insurance Loans, Current Bills

Record the actual debts and loans that need to be paid off in the event of your death. Add to that amount a sum equal to two or three months of average household bills. This will allow your family a few months after your death to get reorganized.

Income Tax Liabilities

Uncle Sam has little sympathy. In the year of your death, there will still be income tax liabilities. If your beneficiaries are required to take payouts from your various retirement plans, pension plans, profit-sharing plans, IRAs, Keogh Plans, tax sheltered annuity plans, and non-qualified deferred annuities, they must pay income taxes on those distributions. Such income taxes will diminish the value of these assets by as much as one third or more. Your CPA is best qualified to assist you in calculating the potential income tax as a result of these distributions, and also to advise you on how to reduce income tax obligations. If the assets under such plans are substantial, your beneficiaries will save more money than you will spend to get professional advice on how to distribute these assets most economically to them. Since each beneficiary's income tax situation is different from every other beneficiary, the income tax liability for each will be different. Each one involved will need individual counseling.

The changing tax laws, economy, and tax-sheltered investments (such as limited partnerships) may have caused you problems. Those problems do not cease at death. If you own a tax shelter on which you have borrowed money in excess of your cost basis in that tax shelter and/or the fair market value of that tax shelter, your death will trigger an income tax liability—another of those less-than-pleasant surprises that may occur to your beneficiaries in the event of your death. You may lessen such shocks by making sure sufficient assets are made available to pay the income tax liability and that all records are easily located.

Federal Estate Tax

If everything you own—and we mean *everything*—including the full face amount of your life insurance policies is worth less than $600,000 on the date you die, and the laws are the same then as they are now in 1989, you will not have to worry about federal estate taxes as long as you have not previously used up your $600,000 exemption by giving substantial gifts to people. There is an exemption that allows you to give up to $600,000 to anyone, during your life or at death, and not pay any estate or gift taxes on that transfer. If you are married at the time of your death, you still may give that $600,000 to someone other than your spouse without incurring estate taxes. Also, you may transfer to your spouse an unlimited amount of assets without incurring any estate taxes. Thus, an unlimited amount may pass to a spouse without incurring estate taxes, and $600,000 may pass to someone other than a spouse without incurring gift or estate taxes either during life or at death.

Therefore, if a husband owns $600,000 in assets including the full face amount of life insurance and a wife owns, in her name only, another $600,000 in assets, they could each give $600,000 in assets to anyone they choose without incurring federal estate taxes. It other words, in a husband/wife situation a total of $1.2 million in assets may be paid to surviving non-spousal beneficiaries without federal estate taxes, as long as the estate is arranged to accomplish that objective.

For those of you whose assets total less than $600,000, federal estate taxes are not of concern; you may skip the balance of this section unless you expect your assets to grow to over $600,000.

Those whose property exceeds $600,000 in value, however, must face the fact that Uncle Sam will claim a substantial portion of those assets at your death via the federal estate tax (see Figure 7–5). The percentage of the tax bite goes as high as 55% of the asset value. The problem with federal estate taxes in addition to being very substantial, they are due relatively quickly after your death. Uncle Sam wishes to be paid within nine months of the date of your death, and he wishes to be paid in cash. If your estate is comprised of marketable securities, bank accounts, cash, and so on, the estate may have no difficulty raising that cash in time to pay the bill. However, if your estate is comprised of real estate, a non-public business interest or some other material assets that are not readily convertible to cash, then you have a problem. Consider the consternation of your beneficiaries if they are forced to liquidate your qualified plans, pay an income tax of about one-third of their value, pay estate taxes of up to 55% and possibly a 15% excise tax on any excess in your retirement plans.

There are a number of solutions to these tax problems. The first one is, don't own—if you don't own it, the government can't tax it. That may sound impractical or impossible and at most times of life, it is. However, as people get older, the accumulation of additional assets becomes less important. People discover that what makes them really wealthy is income. Income that is constantly replaced. Income that they can spend today knowing that it will be replaced tomorrow. Income that they are free to spend, enjoy and give, without concern that they won't have enough for tomorrow. When that is attained, the time is appropriate to start giving away assets. The best type of asset to give away is the asset that doesn't yield income but is rapidly appreciating and exacerbating estate tax liability problems. It is well worth your money to obtain competent advisors such as your attorney, CPA, trust officer and life insurance professional, who will help you accomplish your objectives and minimize estate taxes through an appropriate gifting program and proper legal documents. There is concern among these professionals that your ability to give away $600,000 of your assets either during life or at death will be legislated out of existence or reduced in the near future. If this is true, it could cost the owner of a substantial estate $50,000 in taxes for every $100,000 reduction in the ex-

Figure 7–5
Unified Transfer Tax Rate Schedule

The unified rate schedule applying to estates of people dying after 1976 (and gifts made after 1976) appears below.

Column A Taxable amount over	Taxable amount not over	Tax on amount in column A	Rate of tax on excess over amount in column A (percent)
0	$ 10,000	0	18
$ 10,000	20,000	$ 1,800	20
20,000	40,000	3,800	22
40,000	60,000	8,200	24
60,000	80,000	13,000	26
80,000	100,000	18,200	28
100,000	150,000	23,800	30
150,000	250,000	38,800	32
250,000	500,000	70,800	34
500,000	750,000	155,800	37
750,000	1,000,000	248,300	39
1,000,000	1,250,000	345,800	41
1,250,000	1,500,000	448,300	43
1,500,000	2,000,000	555,800	45
$2,500,000	$3,000,000	$1,025,800	53
3,000,000	————	1,290,800	55

Source: *U.S. Master Tax Guide, 72nd Edition*, by Commerce Clearing House Inc., 1989 Guide

emption approved by Congress. If this concerns you, see your advisors now and arrange to take advantage of that $600,000 exemption as soon as is possible and practical. It is likely that your gift, made prior to the change in this law, would be grandfathered.

Charitable Remainder Trusts

There is a way to give something away for estate tax purposes, but to keep the income from what you have given away for yourself. A piece of property may be considered two pieces instead of one: part one is the income interest in the property, part two is the "remainder" interest or what is left when you die. The second part may be given to charity while you retain part one for yourself.

Although you may think it would be difficult to determine the value of these two parts of one piece of property, it is not because the IRS issues valuation tables based on life expectancy and interest rates that must be used.

If you want to give to your favorite charity, but also want income for your life, or for your own and your spouse's life, the best item to give would be an asset which you obtained at very low cost (low cost basis). It should be an asset that has appreciated rapidly and will continue to do so, thus increasing estate taxes in the future while generating little or no income for you currently. Your objective in giving this asset to charity is to increase income, decrease future estate taxes, enjoy a current deduction for a charitable contribution and earn the appreciation of the charitable organization now rather than posthumously.

The key to this strategy is that you can give this highly appreciated asset to charity and the charity can sell it, invest the total proceeds without paying any capital gains tax whatsoever. They can reinvest the proceeds to generate income which they will pay to you. If you sold the appreciated asset personally, you would have to pay capital gains taxes of about 30% which would have netted you 30%, less capital available to generate income than is available to the charity.

For example, if you sold something for a $100,000 profit, you could assume that the state and federal government taxes would total 30% on the $100,000 profit—you would net $70,000 to invest. Assuming an interest rate of 6%, your income would be $4,200 per year. However, if you donated that $100,000 asset to charity, the charity could sell the asset, pay nothing to the state and federal government, put the full

$100,000 to work for you, earn 6% and pay you $6,000 per year. Your income would increase by more than 42%.

Some people are reluctant to do this because the gift deprives their personal beneficiaries of the value of the asset at their eventual death. However, it is entirely possible that the additional income provided by the charity would be enough to allow you to gift a part of it to your beneficiaries (as present interest gifts which qualify for the $10,000 per person, per year annual exemption), who could then buy life insurance on your life or, in a husband and wife situation, buy a "second to die" life insurance policy. These policies may be used to provide cash to replace the value of the asset you gave to charity in what is called a "wealth replacement trust". Since ownership of the trust would not be held by you or your spouse, it would not be included in your estate at your own or your spouse's death. In addition, you would have a current charitable deduction for the present value of the remainder interest you give to the charity.

Discuss this arrangement with your favorite charity, attorney, accountant and life insurance professional. It can be well worth the effort.

This can be a situation in which everybody wins. You reduce your estate taxes and income taxes while receiving more income during your life. The charity receives a future gift; and Uncle Sam, while sacrificing tax revenues, helps a charity remain economically healthy, doing what society might have to do otherwise.

Marital Deduction

If the "don't own" solution is not practical in your case, yet you are worried about substantial estate taxes and the fact that the assets within your estate could not be easily liquidated for cash within nine months, then you can eliminate estate taxes by making sure that you are married on the day you die. You leave all your assets to your surviving spouse. The so-called "marital deduction" allows you to pass to your spouse unlimited assets at death, free from any estate taxes.

Two things make this strategy difficult. The first may be that not all of your assets should pass to your spouse but should pass to other beneficiaries. The second is that estate taxes are not avoided, but simply deferred until your spouse's death.

The strategy of leaving all assets to the surviving spouse at the death of the first spouse will work once. It will not work at the death of that surviving spouse who, as a single individual, will no longer qualify for any marital deduction. Any estate over the $600,000 exemption will be subject to federal estate taxes. Life insurance on an estate owner whose death will create estate tax problems is often a solution for making sure that cash is available to pay taxes.

Second To Die Life Insurance

A strategy now being used with greater frequency is for the estate owner and spouse to minimize estate taxes at the first death as much as possible. This involves using the marital deduction and the $600,000 exemption to eliminate estate taxes entirely on up to $1,200,000 in assets. Estates larger than this, or unplanned estates, probably face inevitable estate taxes. In order to make sure that cash is available at the second death, a second to die policy (also called a survivorship life policy) may be purchased. Such a policy will not pay off at the death of the first of the two to die, but rather at the second death. As a result, this type of life insurance requires lower premiums than a regular life insurance policy. It also allows a couple, one of whom may not be in the best of health, to obtain life insurance that will pay off in the event of the second death, whereas they might not otherwise qualify medically for regular first to die life insurance.

This is a single-purpose policy. Its objective is to maximize death benefits at the second death. Policies available presently are not the type that you would use during life for their living values or retirement income purposes. Their specific purpose is to provide funds to pay estate taxes *for* an estate, rather than *from* an estate.

If the estate owner or the spouse of the estate owner possess this policy, the full face amount of the death benefit will be includable in the estate and therefore could trigger estate taxes as high as 55% against the total death benefit. This is hardly an appropriate arrangement. The primary benefit of this policy is to the survivors of the estate owner and spouse. If it is sufficient in amount to pay all taxes, it will allow the survivors to take the full value of the assets willed to them at death, rather than splitting those assets with Uncle Sam. Thus, the estate owner and spouse's beneficiaries are the obvious and appropriate purchasers and owners of such a policy. If these beneficiaries purchase and pay for the policy, most appropriately within some kind of a living trust arrangement, the cash to pay the estate taxes will come into their hands at the exact time the taxes are due, at the death of the surviving spouse. The beneficiaries may use the cash from the life insurance proceeds to buy the estate assets, thus providing the estate with cash to pay federal estate taxes. This is a most efficient and economical method of making sure cash is available to pay these taxes. The second to die policy offerings are improving. Currently there are whole life and universal life varieties. In the near future we hope to see a universal variable variety that will make the policies within a family trust very efficient providers for many family purposes—gifting programs, college educations for grandchildren, and so on. (The varieties of life insurance are explained in Chapter Eight.)

State Inheritance Taxes

State inheritance taxes are unique to each state. The federal government allows a credit up to a certain amount if you are required to pay that amount to your state in inheritance taxes. Most state governments then require that you pay them whatever amount the federal government will give you credit for. It makes little difference to you whether the taxes must be sent to the federal government or to the state. Although state inheritance taxes in most states are generally less of a concern than federal estate taxes, they cannot be ignored. Work with your estate advisors to plan your estate and minimize all taxes.

Education Funds

Many readers may be familiar with "the rule of 72." This rule states that 72 divided by a particular interest rate will yield the length of time required for money to double at that particular interest rate. For example, if the interest rate you were considering was 10%, you divide 72 by 10% and determine that money compounded at 10% would double in 7.2 years. Similarly, if your child's college education costs $10,000 per year today, and you expect education costs to escalate at 10%, we must expect educational costs to increase to $20,000 per year in approximately 7.2 years.

In calculating what you will need for college education funds, consider what it would cost to send that child to college at the present time. The instructions for your survivors would be to segregate this sum from your total estate and invest it in a fund that ideally would earn at least enough to keep pace with yearly increases in education costs, generating sufficient funds to provide for the child's college education. The more conservative you are, the larger your fund at the outset. Enter your estimate in the inventory in the blank provided for education funds.

Mortgage Funds

As you consider your estimate for money required to pay off mortgages, you may decide that you prefer, and that it would be more sensible economically, not to pay off the mortgages. Your survivors must then be able to service the mortgage; that is, they must be able to pay the principle, interest, taxes, insurance and other property maintenance costs. Make sure that your beneficiaries have the flexibility to achieve this. It is wise to have a mortgage fund so that your beneficiaries and their counsel may debate the merits of either position—paying off the mortgage or continuing the mortgage—from a position of economic strength rather than from a position of economic weakness. Provide the funds to pay off mortgages if they choose to do so.

Family Emergency Fund

Even though you have done your best to accurately estimate the various cash funds required at your death, invariably you will be wrong. The function of the family emergency fund is to make sure that your errors are not economically devastating to your survivors. We normally recommend a family emergency fund of six months' gross income. Many people gasp at this amount; however, if we call it instead an emergency/opportunity fund and remind people of the times in their lives that they were forced to pass up a good opportunity because they didn't have sufficient liquid cash to take advantage of it, they understand our recommendation. If you have six months' gross income and an outstanding opportunity comes along, you will not mind risking up to one-half of the amount on the opportunity because you know that a basic emergency fund of three months' gross income remains.

The figures that you enter in Figure 7–3 are your demands for cash for your family in the event of your death. They represent what you perceive as economic security to your family. If all of these specific funds are provided for, your next concern would be the monthly income needed by your survivors to provide for their day-to-day living.

Survivor Income Funds

The need for survivor income funds is obviously dependent upon the economic circumstances of the survivors. If you leave a spouse who is every bit as capable of earning income as you are, with no surviving children dependent upon that survivor, then survivor income funds may be unnecessary. Your standard of living, we assume, has not increased to such an extent that two incomes are needed to maintain either you or your spouse. In many families today there is only one income earner, and the family's economic survival is dependent upon that individual's continued earnings. In this case, the need for a survivor income fund is obvious. A survivor income fund is also needed in two-earner families where the family's standard of living requires both earnings to pay the bills and mortgages, and maintain the family.

Annuity Method

When considering the income funds needed for a family, we define three basic time periods, as shown in Figure 7–6. The first covers the period of time until the youngest child attains age eighteen. The second is the period between the youngest child's age eighteen and the spouse's age sixty. The final period goes from the spouse's age sixty for the rest of life which is estimated to be to age eighty-five. We use these three periods because of the way social security payments are made—they are payable to the families of workers while children up to eighteen years of age are being cared for. Benefits then cease and are no longer payable until the surviving spouse reaches age sixty.

Period One

The spouse of a deceased worker will receive a benefit personally up until the youngest child attains age sixteen. Child's benefit continue until age eighteen. We use $300 per eligible beneficiary as a rule-of-thumb (ROT) benefit for social security, with a maximum of three per family. This is an inaccurate, but conservative, number. Should you wish to use more accurate numbers, you may obtain a table of benefits from the Social Security Administration, or better yet request from them a report on your benefits. A form is available from your local social security office which you should complete and send in at least once every three years to verify that your account with Social Security is accurate.

Figure 7–6
Life Insurance Needs Analyzer—Survivor Income Funds

	Number Childred	Years of Income	Monthly Income
INCOME PERIODS:			
1. Children Under 18	_____	_____	_____
2. Children Over 18, Spouse Under 60/65	_____	_____	_____
3. Spouse Age 60/65 For Life (Recommended Age 85)	_____	_____	_____

PERIOD 1 INCOME OBJECTIVE $ _____
Less: 1. Est. Social Security*   _____
       2. Spouse's Earned Income   _____
       3. Other Assured Income   _____
Net Unfunded Income Objective   _____ per month
Discounted Present Value
for _____ Years   _____
Assuming _____ Interest $ Child Raising Fund
* (ROT : Social Security Benefits—$300 per Eligible Beneficiary, Maximum 3)

PERIOD 2 INCOME OBJECTIVE $ _____
Less: 1. Est. Social Security*   _____
       2. Spouse's Earned Income   _____
       3. Other Assured Income   _____
Net Unfunded Income Objective   _____ per month
* Social Security Benefits STOP

Discounted Present Value
for _____ Years   _____
Assuming _____ Interest $ Post Children Fund

PERIOD 3 INCOME OBJECTIVE $ _____
Less: 1. Est. Social Security   _____
       2. Spouses Earned Income   _____
       3. Other Assured Income   _____
       4. IRA & Other Ret. Plans   _____
Net Unfunded Income Objective $ _____ per month
* (ROT : Social Security Benefits—$600 per Month)

Discounted Present Value
for _____ Years   _____
Assuming _____ Interest $ Retirement Fund

ANNUITY METHOD FOR INCOME IN THE EVENT OF DEATH $ _____
(Principle ZERO ($0) at Spouse's Life Expectancy)

ALTERNATE METHOD—CAPITAL RETENTION METHOD $ _____
Assuming _____ % Interest   _____
(Principle _____ at Spouse's Life Expectancy)

ROT = Rule of Thumb

Social security income could be supplemented by the spouse's own continuing income. Remember that a spouse's earnings in excess of a certain threshold may reduce or eliminate social security benefits. However, if the spouse is capable and desirous of earning substantially more than the threshold amount, this is, of course, advisable. The third item providing for the spouse's continuing income is any miscellaneous source that may be available to that spouse. Record these three sources in the spaces provided on Figure 7–6, and compare them to your income objective. Is there any unfunded income objective remaining? If there is, funds need to be made available to provide for it. Knowing the amount of income required and the time period during which it is required, we usually use a 6% assumed interest rate and discount that required stream of income to its present value. The lump sum calculated will provide sufficient capital so that a monthly income may be paid from that capital sum to the surviving spouse during the required period of time. At the end of that period of time, both the capital sum and the 6% interest it earned will have been used up. A zero balance will remain at the end of the payment period which is why this is referred to as the "Annuity Method."

Period Two

Period two is unique. During this period—in which children are over age eighteen and the surviving spouse is under age sixty—no social security benefits are payable. The only support for the spouse during this period is earned income and other miscellaneous income which may be available. Of course, at this time, the spouse will have fewer parental responsibilities and will be freer to seek a career and a higher income job. During this second period the objective may be to provide just enough supplemental income to allow the surviving spouse to terminate an unsatisfying position and/or to take the time to obtain the education required to get a better-paying position. The amount of funds required for this period is calculated in the same way shown for period one: take the amount of monthly income desired for the number of years it is desired and discount that stream of income at 6% to determine the lump sum required at the beginning of the period. A second step is required in this calculation. The lump sum calculated is not *currently* required—it is required at the time in the future when there are no longer any children under age eighteen. Therefore, we discount the future value lump sum back to the present value using a 6% interest rate and the number of years between the present time and the time when it is required. This will tell us that we will need "x" dollars in the event of your death to be put aside as of the date of death to earn 6% so that your spouse will have the required amount at the beginning of period two. The amount needed at the beginning of period two is the future value; the number of years from the present to the beginning of period two gives us our time factor; and 6% is our interest rate. You will need the help of a financial calculator or a computer to figure this out.

Period Three

Income period three starts when social security becomes available again to the surviving spouse. This can be as early as age sixty. Also at 59 1/2, IRAs and other retirement plan benefits become payable without penalty. And of course, we will have the spouse's earned income and any other assured income that may be available to that individual. Total up these four sources and check their adequacy against your objectives. If they are insufficient to provide for your surviving spouse's standard of living, you will wish to add to them. We refer to this third period as the retirement fund. The calculation for the amount of the retirement fund is similar to that for period two—the discounted present value method. The numbers needed for this calculation are: the amount of income required per month; the time period (twenty-five years times twelve months); and the monthly interest rate (we normally assume 6%, .5% per month). The discounted present value method gives you the lump sum required at the beginning of period three, which begins at your spouse's age sixty. That amount of money becomes the future value in our second calculation. That is the amount of money needed when your spouse attains age sixty—a future value. Six percent is the interest that it can earn. The time is from the present to the spouse's age 60. You will need "x" amount of money to make sure the lump sum is available at the beginning of the retirement period so that the amount of income you specified may be paid out for the twenty-five years we expect your surviving spouse to live. At the termination of that time, no funds will remain.

This is referred to as the *annuity method* of providing income in the event of death. When the surviving spouse attains the age of 85, the principal and income will have been entirely used up; there will be no capital remaining. One advantage of this system is that the survivor will not have any estate taxes. The disadvantage of the annuity method is that not everyone dies at 85. (My 82-year-old mother thinks it is definitely a dumb idea!)

Capital Retention Method

An alternate method for determining how much capital you would like to have for your surviving spouse is referred to as the *capital retention method*. The capital retention method assumes that you will not invade principal: you will use *only the interest* on the funds to provide income. In order to calculate the amount required for your survivors under this method, review the incomes required for periods one, two and three. Pick the highest income required for any of the three periods. For example, if the highest income required from supplemental funds in any of the three periods was $1,000 per month ($12,000 per year), how much capital at 6% would be required to generate $12,000 per year income without invading principal? By dividing $12,000 by our interest rate assumption of 6%, you will find that you need $200,000 in capital to generate $12,000 a year in income at 6%. That $200,000 worth of capital could generate that income right from the start, through all three periods, and never diminish its principal. If some income periods require less than that, then the surviving spouse is more than adequately provided for, can reinvest the excess income and can work on protecting her income stream from reductions in purchasing power due to inflation. The effects of inflation can be provided for further by adding to capital all earnings in excess of the 6% rate, so that the capital base from which the 6% is being used grows. If you are more concerned about inflation, assume a lower assured interest rate and provide sufficient capital to do the job at the lower assumed rate. The surviving spouse may add to capital any earnings in excess of that assumption. It takes discipline, but it works. When you compare this $200,000 requirement under the capital retention method, meaning that the 85-year-old will still have $200,000 of capital rather than no capital, you may be surprised that the amount of capital required for the annuity method is not much less than the $200,000 required for the capital retention method. The younger you are, the more true this is. The reason for this is the "Pac-Man effect" of a fund that is paying out both principal and interest. Every time principal is paid out, there is less left to earn interest; thus, more principal must be paid out in the succeeding year, so less interest is earned—all principal is quickly dissipated. It is compound interest in reverse. For this reason it is suggested that you avoid the annuity method.

Inflation

Inflation is always a problem when you estimate future survivor income needs. The $1,000 per month that you estimate will be required will purchase less in the future as prices increase. It therefore will become inadequate to the extent that inflation erodes purchasing power. In order to offset this risk then, your surviving spouse must be able to increase the capital base from which she or he is taking income by an amount equal to inflation each year.

This means, of course, that the surviving spouse is not going to be able to take the capital left at the first spouse's death, put it into a savings account and spend all the interest. That capital must be invested carefully and diversified if it is to provide family security for a long period of time. Often, a spouse will need assistance in doing this, and it is readily available in the trust departments of banks and from other investment advisors. A great deal of care should be taken in choosing such assistance, because this is a matter of family survival money and the survivors cannot ignore its management. Inattention will create the highest risk of loss.

If you are greatly concerned with inflation, you will want to reduce the interest rates that you have used in calculating the amount of capital needed for your surviving spouse. For example, if you feel that long-term inflation rates are going to average 4% and you feel that the funds made available to your surviving spouse can generate 8%, you will want to use 4 % (the difference between the 8% earned and 4% inflation) rather than the 6% used in the discounted value problems as the assumed interest rate on capital. A reduction in assumed interest rate will increase the amount of capital required. The spouse will then live on 4% and the remaining 4% may be reinvested in order to increase the capital base, and therefore provide more capital to generate more future income.

Comparing What You Need To What You Have

In Figure 7–3 you have calculated the cash sums your family will need, and in Figure 7–6 the capital sums required (by the annuity method and the capital sum method) to provide survivor income. The cash sum and income fund sum combined equals your total cash requirement for your family, which is to be recorded at the top of Figure 7–7.

Now that you have determined the total amount of capital your family needs in the event of your death as per your personal specifications, you may start subtracting what you have already accumulated for their benefit, such as your present invested capital, the net benefits of your life insurance and the cash generated by your retirement funds. The difference between what you decided was required and what you have accumulated is your shortage or surplus. The most immediate way to provide for that shortage is to pay a premium for a life insurance policy with a face amount equal

---

Figure 7–7
Life Insurance Needs Analyzer—Survivor Income Funds

TOTAL FAMILY CAPITAL REQUIRED FOR EXPENSES & INCOME:

	Annuity	Capital
Less:		
1 Present Family Investment Capital	_____	
2. Existing Net Benefits of Life Insurance	_____	
3. Retirement Plan Generated Cash	_____	
	-_____	-_____

ADDITIONAL FAMILY CAPITAL REQUIRED*
or (Surplus) Family Capital Available.

* NOTE: Additional life insurance of this amount, assuming _____ % interest, would create sufficient dollars for your estate to accomplish all of your stated family objectives. Listed above.

---

to what you are lacking in capital. Once the insurance company has accepted you as an insured and issued your policy, that total amount of capital is immediately available at your death for your family's benefit. There is no other economic tool that can do this for you.

To many, the amount of life insurance determined in this manner is the amount they believe provides adequately for their families. Most people round off the amount determined—for example, if it comes out to $228,000, you'll probably want $250,000 worth of life insurance, if it comes out to $450,000, you'll want $500,000 of insurance; if it comes to $900,000 you'll probably want $1 million. Whatever the amount, remember that it represents family security. It lets you and your spouse sleep comfortably, satisfied that your family will not become wards of the state in the event of your death.

Protecting Your Family

You've now determined what you need, but nothing is really resolved until you take action. It's your family that stands to lose if you die. The insurance company should be taking the risk, not you or your family. Now is not the time to debate what kind of life insurance you should have. Now *is* the time to put a policy in force. Assuming that you are dealing with a quality insurance company, our recommendation to you would be to buy a yearly renewable and convertible term policy. This means that you will pay the insurance company the amount necessary to pay the mortality and expenses on a policy on your life in the amount you've determined is necessary for a one-year period. We recommend this type of policy because it allows you to spend the minimum amount to put a policy in force immediately and protects your family as quickly as possible. You may have opportunities to obtain such life insurance through your employer via group insurance or through some organization that you belong to with association group life insurance. At this point our concern it is not *who* will pay the death benefit in the event of your death, as long as *somebody* will. Put the coverage in force wherever it is most expedient—(and stay healthy until the right coverage can be put in force)! (We spend more time in Chapter 8 determining if the means you have chosen to provide insurance is the best long-term solution for providing for your family's security.)

Getting your policy in force as quickly as possible will not only remove a financial burden from your family, but it will also prepare you for making additional decisions. You will know how much it costs you to own life insurance. You will know the mortality and expense charges required as a result of your age, sex, smoking habits, general health condition and maybe even your occupation. Once this minimum cost has been determined and accepted by you, decisions can be made as to how to finance the payment of these mortality and expense charges. You will find in the next chapter that your decision as to how to best finance the payment of your mortality and expense charges is basically a decision as to what kind of life insurance you want, and it is based upon the availability of funds and your various investment opportunities and objectives with those funds.

The Action Letter in Figure 7–8 may be sent to the insurance company of your choice in order to initiate action. If you have already selected an insurance company and an agent with whom you would like to work, address this issue immediately.

Summary

The objective of this chapter has been to assist you in determining how much life insurance you need, and, to get it in force as quickly as possible with the least amount of financial commitment. Our next question will be, *"is* least best?" Far too many publications answer this question with a resounding "Yes." However, you may find that this may not be true for you.

Figure 7–8
Life Insurance Action Letter

I am evaluating my life insurance and would appreciate your assistance.

I would be interested in your recommendations regarding the type of life insurance I now own, keeping in mind that my principal objective is to own enough to provide adequate security for my survivors at minimum after-tax cost for the protection.

I have not decided whether I need or want any additional life insurance. Please send me a ledger statement showing the cost of $_____ of yearly renewable and convertible term insurance for a male, nonsmoker/smoker, age _____ and $_____ for a female, nonsmoker/smoker, age _____ .

If you have an alternative policy that you would recommend, please send me the information, including a ledger statement for any contract you are recommending. If you will be offering Universal Life or Universal Variable, I will need a statement of monthly charges, mortality cost, credits, account values and surrender values for the first eleven years and a statement disclosing the assumptions being used in the statement.

Sincerely,

Enclosure(s): Declarations pages copies from life insurance policies to be reviewed.

EIGHT

WHAT KIND OF LIFE INSURANCE?

All life insurance policies issued have two common costs—the charges for mortality and expenses. The money paid into a policy is applied to these two costs with any excess held in reserve. If you pay in more than is required for the current year's mortality and expense charges, the surplus is invested for you in an investment account within the policy.

Expense charges are incurred in issuing and managing the policy. Mortality charges or life insurance costs are calculated by the insurance company to cover the amount the life insurance company promised under your policy at your death. The insurance company, in effect, has pooled you with others of your same age, sex, smoking habits and physical make up. You and I don't know if we are going to die next year, but if enough of us are together, the number of people who will die in any one year from among this large group can be predicted with great statistical accuracy. The insurance company has taken an uncertainty on our part, and turned it

143

into a certainty on their part. Therefore, if we all contribute "x" to the fund held by the insurance company, there will be sufficient dollars in the fund to pay the death benefits to those that will die in the coming year. That's the mortality cost, the cost of the "life insurance."

These two, mortality costs and expenses, are a part of *every* life insurance policy. They cannot be avoided or the insurance company would go out of business. You do not want your insurance company going out of business before you do.

We will discuss the amount allocated to investment within the insurance policy in the section on term "plus" insurance.

Term Insurance

Term insurance is the type of insurance for which you pay just the mortality and expense charges, and no more. Typically, the most efficient form of term insurance is yearly renewable and convertible term. With this policy you pay the mortality and expense charges for the current year only, and you accept the fact that as you get older, your mortality costs will go up. In each succeeding year, you can expect the premium on this type of policy to go up.

If you want very inexpensive term insurance, don't ask the insurance company to do anything more than to pay the death benefit. As a result of not having to make any extra promises, the insurance company will be able to minimize your cost. If, however, you want more from the insurance company, such as the promise to accept your premium in the coming years and to allow your insurance to continue (renewable *term insurance*), you will have to pay a little bit extra for that promise of renewability. Most people willingly pay extra for this renewal privilege because you never know when you may go from "insurable" to "uninsurable." Uninsurability may be a result of the deterioration of your health, your latest avocation, or your current occupation. In any case, insurance companies may not wish to provide new life insurance for you at any cost. At that time, that renewal privilege on your existing policies will become particularly important to you.

You also may want to pay for the convertibility feature in a life insurance policy. This allows you to change your term insurance policy into any of the other types of contracts that are issued by the same company that has issued your term insurance policy. This means that if you are dealing with an insurance company that has an incomplete portfolio of products, or does not have the type of product you'll want to replace your term insurance, the convertibility feature is not of value to you. You will want to deal with an insurance company that has a complete portfolio of products and/or at least that type of product that you may wish to use in the future.

There also are term insurance policies which charge a level premium for five years, ten years, even as long as twenty years. The insurance company has taken a look at the yearly renewable and convertible term rate required each year and has averaged it out over the period of time. They then ask you for an average level premium for the five-, ten- or twenty-year period. The disadvantage of this type of policy is that you are paying more than is required in the early years so that you may pay less than is normally required in the future. If you keep the term insurance policy for the total period of time it might be a fair arrangement; however, when the time value of money is taken into consideration, it usually works to the insurance company's benefit. Also, since many people adjust their term insurance policies from year to year, paying this additional premium in the beginning of the period when you may not own the policy at the end of the period can be a waste of money.

You also can buy a term insurance policy with a level premium, but the death benefit will be reduced each year so that the same premium is sufficient to cover the mortality and expense charges that exist during that particular year. This is commonly referred to as *decreasing term insurance*. The insurance companies like to market it as mortgage insurance to make you feel as if you need to buy it. This type of insurance puts the insurance company in control of reducing the amount of your death benefit each year. To put yourself in control you could buy a level yearly renewable and convertible term insurance policy and then, in the coming years, if you decide that you do not need that amount of life insurance, *you* ask the insurance company to reduce the face amount.

When insurance companies put term life insurance in force, they must estimate expenses and the number of people who are going to die. Actual results will inevitably differ from these estimates. If the difference is in favor of the insurance company, mutual insurance companies will return that excess to the policyowner in the form of dividends. To some extent, dividends can be controlled by the insurance company by estimating mortality and expenses conservatively or aggressively. A mutual company that conservatively estimates mortality and expenses plays it safe. They estimate that more people will die and expenses will be high. They charge more, but promise to lower costs by paying dividends if they find that their estimates have been too conservative.

An insurance company can price aggressively by paring down estimates, calculating as closely as possible, and charging you as little as possible for mortality and expenses. In order to protect themselves, they will specify in the contract that if they have charged you significantly less than the mortality and expenses actually incurred, they can, in the future, raise your rates. Formerly, conservative estimates used to be the norm—that is, term rates used to be estimated high and the high rates were reduced by returning dividends to the insured. Today, the norm is to rate life insurance policies aggressively and reserve the right to increase costs.

This latter method provides you, the consumer, with a cash flow advantage. It is like receiving your dividends up front. Also, the insurance companies will work very hard to maintain low rates in their term insurance policies and avoid increasing rates for competitive reasons. The maximum rates listed in the policies set the limits on what the insurance companies can charge you for mortality and expenses. The maximum mortality rates that you will find in today's life insurance policies will be based upon the 1980 Commissioners Standard Ordinary (1980 CSO) mortality table, which indicates the number of deaths per thousand to be expected in each particular age group. The table is shown in Figure 8–1. In all likelihood, you will find that these rates are more than your actual payments to your life insurance company.

Life Insurance Policy Types

Figure 8–2, the Product Analyzer, summarizes the generic forms of life insurance in a matrix that describes the basic features of each policy. The policy that appeals to you will depend upon your life insurance needs, your economic situation, and your likes and dislikes in regard to the various types of investments available within an insurance company and an insurance policy. At the end of this chapter is a suitability questionnaire (Figure 8–4) which will assist you in deciding which policy is best suited to you at the present time. It is used with the permission of the Financial Products Standards Board, Inc. for whom it was developed.

Refer to the Product Analyzer while you fill out the Suitability Questionnaire. Once this process is complete, you should be able to make a personal choice as to what policy or policies suit you best.

The objective of the Suitability Questionnaire is to see that you understand the life insurance products available and are aware of the costs of life insurance. Life insurance is a consumable commodity which is paid for each year. Its cost must be extracted from your investment earnings or your payment, depending upon the method of payment you have chosen. The election to invest or not to invest additional cash into a life insurance policy is a voluntary decision. The decision should be based upon the availability of investment capital and the appropriateness of the particular investment media within the life insurance contract to meet your investment needs, personal goals and objectives. Once you've made your decision regarding which of the six generic forms of life insurance is appropriate for you, you may then select a contract based upon more quantitative analysis of expenses, mortality

Figure 8–1
1980 Commissioners Standard Ordinary Mortality Table

Age	Male Mortality Rate Per 1,000	Male Expectancy, Years	Female Mortality Rate Per 1,000	Female Expectancy, Years	Age	Male Mortality Rate Per 1,000	Male Expectancy, Years	Female Mortality Rate Per 1,000	Female Expectancy, Years
0	4.18	70.83	2.89	75.83	50	6.71	25.36	4.96	29.53
1	1.07	70.13	.87	75.04	51	7.30	24.52	5.31	28.67
2	.99	69.20	.81	74.11	52	7.96	23.70	5.70	27.82
3	.98	68.27	.79	73.17	53	8.71	22.89	6.15	26.98
4	.95	67.34	.77	72.23	54	9.56	22.08	6.61	26.14
5	.90	66.40	.76	71.28	55	10.47	21.29	7.09	25.31
6	.85	65.46	.73	70.34	56	11.46	20.51	7.57	24.49
7	.80	64.52	.72	69.39	57	12.49	19.74	8.03	23.67
8	.76	63.57	.70	68.44	58	13.59	18.99	8.47	22.86
9	.74	62.62	.69	67.48	59	14.77	18.24	8.94	22.05
10	.73	61.66	.68	66.53	60	16.08	17.51	9.47	21.25
11	.77	60.71	.69	65.58	61	17.54	16.79	10.13	20.44
12	.85	59.75	.72	64.62	62	19.19	16.08	10.96	19.65
13	.99	58.80	.75	63.67	63	21.06	15.38	12.02	18.86
14	1.15	57.86	.80	62.71	64	23.14	14.70	13.25	18.08
15	1.33	56.93	.85	61.76	65	25.42	14.04	14.59	17.32
16	1.51	56.00	.90	60.82	66	27.85	13.39	16.00	16.57
17	1.67	55.09	.95	59.87	67	30.44	12.76	17.43	15.83
18	1.78	54.18	.98	58.93	68	33.19	12.14	18.84	15.10
19	1.86	53.27	1.02	57.98	69	36.17	11.54	20.36	14.38
20	1.90	52.37	1.05	57.04	70	39.51	10.96	22.11	13.67
21	1.91	51.47	1.07	56.10	71	43.30	10.39	24.23	12.97
22	1.89	50.57	1.09	55.16	72	47.65	9.84	26.87	12.28
23	1.86	49.66	1.11	54.22	73	52.64	9.30	30.11	11.60
24	1.82	48.75	1.14	53.28	74	58.19	8.79	33.93	10.95
25	1.77	47.84	1.16	52.34	75	64.19	8.31	38.24	10.32
26	1.73	46.93	1.19	51.40	76	70.53	7.84	42.97	9.71
27	1.71	46.01	1.22	50.46	77	77.12	7.40	48.04	9.12
28	1.70	45.09	1.26	49.52	78	83.90	6.97	53.45	8.55
29	1.71	44.16	1.30	48.59	79	91.05	6.57	59.35	8.01
30	1.73	43.24	1.35	47.65	80	98.84	6.18	65.99	7.48
31	1.78	42.31	1.40	46.71	81	107.48	5.80	73.60	6.98
32	1.83	41.38	1.45	45.78	82	117.25	5.44	82.40	6.49
33	1.91	40.46	1.50	44.84	83	128.26	5.09	92.53	6.03
34	2.00	39.54	1.58	43.91	84	140.25	4.77	103.81	5.59
35	2.11	38.61	1.65	42.98	85	152.95	4.46	116.10	5.18
36	2.24	37.69	1.76	42.05	86	166.09	4.18	129.29	4.80
37	2.40	36.78	1.89	41.12	87	179.55	3.91	143.32	4.43
38	2.58	35.87	2.04	40.20	88	193.27	3.66	158.18	4.09
39	2.79	34.96	2.22	39.28	89	207.29	3.41	173.94	3.77
40	3.02	34.05	2.42	38.36	90	221.77	3.18	190.75	3.45
41	3.29	33.16	2.64	37.46	91	236.98	2.94	208.87	3.15
42	3.56	32.26	2.87	36.55	92	253.45	2.70	228.81	2.85
43	3.87	31.38	3.09	35.66	93	272.11	2.44	251.51	2.55
44	4.19	30.50	3.32	34.77	94	295.90	2.17	279.31	2.24
45	4.55	29.62	3.56	33.88	95	329.96	1.87	317.32	1.91
46	4.92	28.76	3.80	33.00	96	384.55	1.54	375.74	1.56
47	5.32	27.90	4.05	32.12	97	480.20	1.20	474.97	1.21
48	5.74	27.04	4.33	31.25	98	657.98	.84	655.85	.84
49	6.21	26.20	4.63	30.39	99	1000.00	.50	1000.00	.50

Based on experience of years 1970-1975.

Figure 8-2
Baldwin Financial Systems Product Analyzer

	General Description	Investment Vehicle	Investment Flexibility	Premium Flexibility	Face Amount Flexibility	Appropriate For
	TERM—Mortality & Expenses ONLY					
Non-Guaranteed Term	Lowest Cost Poor Quality	NONE	N/A	NONE Increases Yearly	NONE	Very Limited Situations
Yearly Renewable and Convertible Term	Quality Term After Tax Life Insurance	NONE	N/A	NONE Increases Yearly	NONE	Limited Cash Flow Temporary Needs Protection NOW
	TERM "PLUS"—Mortality & Expenses "PLUS" ADDITIONAL DOLLARS FOR INVESTMENT					
Whole Life	Tried and True Basic Coverage Dividends Make It Great	Insurance Co. Selected Long-term Bonds and Mortgages	NONE To Change Investment of Capital, Borrowing from the Policy and Reinvesting Is Required	NONE Billed Premium Remains Level. Dividends Can Provide Reduction or Elimination. Loans Available.	NONE If You Want More, You Buy New, IF You Can Pass a Physical	The Conservative Older Insureds Substandard Insureds

Figure 8–2 (continued)

	General Description	Investment Vehicle	Investment Flexibility	Premium Flexibility	Face Amount Flexibility	Appropriate For
Universal Life	How Much Would You Like to Pay . . . When?	Annual Interest Sensitive Investments.	**NONE** To Change Investment of Capital Requires WITHDRAWAL of Capital.	**MAXIMUM** Just Enough for. Mortality and Expenses, or AS MUCH AS LAW ALLOWS.	Increase It or Decrease It as Suits Your Life Setting. . . . Stay Healthy for Major Increases.	Younger Insureds Varable Needs Like Short-Term Interest Rate Investments.
Variable Life	We will put it where You want it.	Common Stock Bond Funds Guaranteed Interest Rates Zero Coupons Money Markets etc., etc. . . .	You Name It. You Split It. You Move It. You Borrow It. Both Fixed and Variable Rates.	**NONE** Billed premium remains level. Loans available..	**NONE** If You Want More, You Buy New, IF You Can Pass a Physical.	The Investor. An Alternative to Buy Term. Invest Difference.
Universal Variable Life	**"You Decide!"** How much . . . Where . . . When?	Common Stock Bond Funds Guaranteed Interest Rates Zero Coupons Money Markets etc, etc. . . .	You Name It. You Split It. You Move It. You Withdraw It.	**MAXIMUM** Just Enough for Mortality and Expenses, or AS MUCH AS LAW ALLOWS.	Increase It or Decrease It as Suits Your Life Setting. . . . Stay Healthy for Major Increases.	The Investor. An Alternative to Buy Term. Invest Difference. I Want It MY WAY!

charges, investment alternatives, flexibility, contract provisions, company and service.

Term "Plus"

We have described the various forms of term life insurance. We will now describe all other forms of life insurance as term "plus" since they continue to contain the two basic elements of term insurance, mortality and expense changes, and add to them an investment element, the "plus." Term "plus" life insurance includes whole life, universal life, variable life, and universal variable life insurance.

Consider the following definitions of "invest":

To commit (money) in order to earn a financial return.

Webster's Seventh New Collegiate Dictionary

To put money to use by purchase or expenditure in something offering profitable returns, especially interest or income.

The American College Dictionary

The reason for these two definitions, is that people will periodically argue that it is inappropriate to discuss life insurance and investments together. It is our opinion that the only reason one would put additional money with an insurance company would be to earn a return. You do indeed earn a return on that extra money that goes into a life insurance policy, and what is unique about that return is that it can be used to pay the mortality and expense charges that are within the life insurance contract without the imposition of income taxes. The earnings on your investment within the contract are not subject to current income taxes. The fact that you may purchase a consumable commodity—the mortality and expense charges of a life insurance policy—with pre-tax earnings and currently use that commodity to protect your beneficiaries, is unique to life insurance and is frequently overlooked and underutilized.

Is Life Insurance a Good Investment?

Is life insurance a good investment or not? The answer is, it depends. For example, suppose you put $1,000 into a life insurance policy that had a $101,000 death benefit. At the end of the year, you received a report from your insurance company that said that the account balance remaining in the policy was $1,000. Some would say this is a terrible investment—the $1,000 earned absolutely nothing during that year. The fact that the policy would have paid $101,000 if you died during that year was, to this individual, totally irrelevant. In this case, for this investor, it was not a good investment.

However, another individual who is paying $100 per year for a $100,000 yearly renewable and convertible term policy would realize that he had received $100 worth of goods and services from the insurance company. He had purchased $100,000 worth of life insurance for the year from the tax-free earnings on the investment within the policy. He bought a needed commodity with pre-tax dollars rather than with after-tax dollars. The $100 worth of life insurance was a 10% tax-free return on the $1,000 investment in the contract.

The key fact is, if you want and need life insurance, it can be a wonderful investment. If you don't want life insurance, then the loss of part or all of your investment return to pay mortality and expense charges is a waste.

Whole Life

Prior to 1976, all life insurance policies issued by companies in the United States had the investment portion invested in the general portfolio of the company. The long-term general portfolio of life insurance companies is comprised primarily of long-term bonds and mortgages. The fixed interest rate long-term bonds and mortgages within this investment portfolio earn the prevailing interest rate at the time they are purchased. It was this type of fixed interest portfolio that was exposed to the incredible, rapid increases in interest rates that brought the prime rate up to 21 ½% by December of 1980. In that environment, a mortgage note or a long-term bond with a 5%, 6%, 7% or 8% interest rate decreased in value as alternative interest rates went up. Who wanted to earn 5% when you could suddenly get 15%? Investors would not pay par value for the old 5% bond when other bonds were paying 15%. The 5% bond could only be sold if the purchase price was decreased, so that the 5% coupon was equal to the 15% return. Figure 8–2 shows the expected selling price of 5% or 9% coupon bonds based upon the level of current interest rates. It dramatically shows the market risk one takes when purchasing long-term bonds.

It was at this point that the Federal Trade Commission chose to examine insurance company investments. Considering the economic environment, it's not surprising that their well-publicized report said that life insurance was providing a poor return on investment. However, while interest rates were high the insurance companies were doing exactly what everyone else was doing. They were working very hard to get as much money invested on a long-term basis at the highest interest rates available. Since that time, interest rates, generally speaking, have come down. The long-term bonds and mortgages that insurance companies were able to put on the books during that time are yielding superior returns. As a result, many of the old whole life policies generate very credible dividends, resulting in reasonable rates of return.

Figure 8–3
Market Risk In Long-Term Bonds

Face Amount	Coupon Rate	Coupon	Market Interest Rate	Market Value
$10,000	5%	$500	5%	$10,000
$10,000	5%	$500	15%	$ 3,333
$10,000	9%	$900	9%	$10,000
$10,000	9%	$900	7%	$12,857

Until 1976, whole life insurance policies that invested in the long-term bonds and mortgages of the general accounts of insurance companies were the only investment type of policy available in the United States. Your policy may have been called a family policy, a life paid up at 65 policy, an endowment policy, a ten- or twenty-pay year life policy, or even a single pay life policy. The names described how long you paid the fixed premium required by, and unique to, whole life insurance. Each policy was issued with a fixed face amount and a fixed annual premium. Whole life insurance policies pass investment results through to the policyowner by way of dividends. These dividends are considered to be a return of premium. The insurance company collects more than is necessary and therefore returns the excess to the policyowner. These dividends are not taxable like dividends received on common stock. They are free of income taxation as long as the total dividends paid do not exceed the total premiums paid into the policy. Prior to the 1980s, this was not likely to occur; today it is likely to occur in policies that you have owned for a long time.

Stock versus Mutual Life Insurance Companies

Your whole life policy may have been issued by a stock insurance company as opposed to a mutual insurance company. The difference between the two is that a stock company is owned by its stockholders, and favorable investment returns, favorable expense experience, and lower mortality experience benefit the stockholders. In a mutual insurance company which is owned by the policyowners, these gains are passed through to the policyowners by way of dividends. The premiums for stock company whole life policies were usually lower than the premium for an equal amount of insurance with a mutual insurance company. During those early years, stock companies stressed the advantage of the "guaranteed" premium that started out lower. However, as interest rates rose in the 1980s, the returns within these policies also increased. Mutual policyowners with whole life policies enjoy those higher returns since they are passed through to them in dividends. Owners of stock whole life policies have no way in which they can receive these same favorable investment results. As a result, whole life insurance issued by stock insurance companies has now become practically extinct. Most people who have had the opportunity to trade their policies have done so. Healthy people with non-participating policies from stock companies may be able to obtain alternative policies that are more economical. They should examine their opportunities to exercise a 1035 tax-free exchange (to be explained later) for an alternative life insurance policy.

Generically speaking, a whole life insurance policy may be described as a policy that has within it charges for expenses and mortality and additional funds invested into the long-term bond and mortgage portfolio of the insurance company. It is a policy which has a fixed premium and a fixed face amount.

Variable Life Insurance

In 1977, the first variable life insurance policy was introduced in the United States by the Equitable Life Assurance Society. Essentially, the insurance company created this policy by changing the investment vehicle available within the contract. They removed the long-term bond and mortgage account and replaced it with two accounts, a common stock account and a money market account. They gave the policyowner the option to use either one or both, and to change back and forth between the two. This was the first-generation variable life policy. This policy, just like its predecessor, whole life insurance, had a fixed premium and a fixed face amount. If you wanted more life insurance, you had to buy another contract. If you couldn't pay the premiums when due, the policy would lapse, value that had accrued in the policy would revert to a fixed life policy under the non-forfeiture provisions available within the contract or default into what is referred to as paid-up extended term insurance. With extended term insurance, the value in the policy is used up buying term insurance for whatever period of time the cash available will sustain. Relative to the investment performance of whole life from 1977 to 1980, this variable whole life policy performed admirably. It showed higher cash value increases and better rates of return for the policyowner than comparable whole life contracts, assuming that the policyowner had the assets invested in the common stock account, despite the fact that the stock market during those years was not at all a great place to be.

Universal Life Insurance—The Product that Changed All Life Insurance

In late 1979 and early 1980, universal life insurance was introduced. Universal life insurance was the life insurance companies' direct response to the demands of the consumer for the high interest rates of the time. Insurance companies decided to use relatively short-term investments and to promise policyowners a stipulated rate of interest for a one-year period commencing on the date they purchased their policy. The interest rates of the early 1980s were high, money markets were popular, and these policies immediately became popular as well.

The insurance company promised policyowners a stipulated rate of return for a year. The policyowners naturally wanted to be able to verify that they actually were receiving the promised rate of return and so did the regulators. As a result, it was necessary for the insurance company to display to the policyowner, for the first time, the monies in the life insurance contract that were necessary to pay the expenses and the mortality charges required by the contract. The day this happened, all life insurance changed. For the first time, a life insurance policy was transparent. You could now see interest earnings and mortality costs. Prior to that time all that anyone had ever seen were the end results, without a breakdown of exactly what was going on inside of the policy each month and each year. Total disclosure became a reality in life insurance with universal life. The impact of this total disclosure on improving the quality of life insurance products for the consumer has yet to be fully realized by consumers and salespeople.

Not only did universal life bring total disclosure to life insurance, it also brought flexibility to life insurance policies. Whole life dictated to the policyowner a fixed face amount, a fixed annual premium and a fixed investment vehicle. Variable life had the fixed minimum face amount and fixed premium; however, it gave the policyowner flexibility of investment vehicle. Universal life eliminated the fixed premium and fixed face amount but, for the moment, offered no flexibility in investment vehicle.

Universal life provides the policyowner with an annual report in which three columns are presented—the expense column, the mortality column and the interest column. If the policyowner wants to increase the death benefit, it may be done by increasing the charges in the mortality column and/or the expense column to the extent necessary for the increase. Reversing that process, if the policyowner wants to reduce the death benefit, the mortality charges are reduced. Thus universal life offers flexibility of face amount, so that the policyowner can use one policy and increase it or decrease it as his life situation dictates. It also offers flexibility of premium payment. The policyowner can add to the investment in the policy by increasing premium payments, or decrease current investment by choosing not to pay premiums. At a minimum, the policy must have sufficient monies in it to cover the mortality and expense charges. The maximum a policy can accept is stipulated in Section 7702 of the Internal Revenue Code. The ability to increase the investment to the maximum extent permitted by law became a problem to Uncle Sam who, in 1988, decided that life insurance was too good an investment and sought to limit the tax benefits of life insurance. This is covered in Chapter 9.

Universal Variable Life Insurance

The next inevitable step in the evolution of the life insurance came about in 1985. Policies that combined universal life that offered flexibility of premium payment and flexibility of face amount but no flexibility of investment were combined with variable life that offered flexibility of investment. In these new universal variable policies, policyowners are given personal control over the life insurance policy's face amount, amount of premium and types of investment. All three basic features are now controlled by the policyowner. Such control makes these policies very unlike the whole life policies of old. You could throw the whole life policy in the safety deposit box and forget it—as long as the mandated premiums were paid on time, the policy would do whatever it was going to do and the policyowner had very little control over it. Policyowner choices were limited to whether they wanted to borrow on the policy or not borrow which, at the time, had little or no impact on the investment results of their own policy. The policyowner could also choose to leave the dividends in the policy or take them out. If you were not enamored with the investment results of the whole life policy, you could withdraw your capital via policy loans and put it elsewhere. That was the limit of control you had over the whole life policies.

Many people did borrow on their policies, particularly at the time that interest rates on money market accounts were going up so substantially in the late 70s and early 80s. The insurance policy usually had a fixed interest rate within it of 5%, 6% or at most 8%, guaranteed by contract. During those years, it paid to borrow on your policy, deduct all the interest while you were in a high tax bracket and deposit the borrowed money in a higher interest bearing account. However, most insurance policy loans are only 20% deductible in 1989, will only be 10% in 1990 and are going to zero deductibility by 1991. In addition, we have lower marginal tax rates and insurance companies charge you a higher rate of interest on your policy if you borrow against it and also reduce your dividends. Thus policy loans, in most cases, no longer make economic sense when the funds borrowed are to be invested elsewhere to earn a higher return.

Universal variable life insurance gives the policyowner a great deal of control. Policyowner management can make these policies perform extremely well. The policyowner can make decisions not only on face amount but also on levels of funding within the policy (how much the policyowner pays into the contract), and where monies paid into their policies are invested in the policy. With flexibility comes responsibility, and opportunity! Policyowners with universal variable contracts will be well advised to carefully read Chapter 9, which will assist them in managing their policies. They will also benefit by securing the services of a well qualified professional life insurance salesperson to help them maximize the benefits of this type of policy.

Hybrid Policies

A number of hybrid policies have been developed that combine features of the four investment types of policies. For example, policies referred to as adjustable life policies are first-generation universal life policies. Universal life, as you can imagine, takes a rather sophisticated computer tracking system to accept varying policyowner premium payments and varying face amounts of life insurance. If a company had not yet obtained the necessary computer expertise, they would issue adjustable life that required less sophisticated computer equipment and technology. This policy requires that a policyowner submit a written request for any change in the amount to be paid into a policy. Based upon this written request, the company would "adjust" the policy. Paying premium at the lowest premium level, your policy would be similar to a ten-year term policy. If you paid premium at the highest premium payment level, your policy would approximate a ten-pay life policy. A ten-pay life policy is a contract in which all of your investment is invested in the contract within ten years. Thereafter, no additional funds can be accepted by the policy. The written request procedure of adjustable life allowed the insurance company to go back into your policy, reprogram what was being recorded and reissue your policy on the new basis. The computer system servicing the policy does not have to be very sophisticated because the paper request gives time for reprogramming. Insurance companies prefer adjustable policies to universal life because they think that you will be more inclined to keep paying premiums into your policy if you have the semi-compulsive encouragement of a premium notice that requires payment or adjustment.

These "adjustable" policies share some of the flexibility of a universal life policy and frequently use the same kind of investment vehicle that universal life uses, that is, a guaranteed interest return for one policy year followed by renewal rates, depending upon market and insurance company conditions.

Insurance companies, similar to every other financial institution, want investment coming into the company each and every year. They are positively disposed toward recurring premium policies. Since the adjustable premium policies are less flexible than universal life and require policyowner action to change the billed premium level, adjustable premium policies are more likely to have recurring premiums paid into them than the universal life type of policy. Universal life leaves the payment of premium entirely to the discretion of the policyowner without the necessity of any particular action other than sending, or not sending the money. For consumers who need the encouragement of a billed premium to maintain a healthy investment level in their insurance policies, the rigidity of adjustable life serves a good purpose.

The interest sensitive whole life contract is another of the hybrid policies. This policy takes the fixed face amount and fixed premium level features of whole life and combines them with the investment vehicle used in a universal life policy. For consumers who prefer the annual interest rate guarantee type of investment over the long-term bond and mortgages of whole life insurance, but who still seek a fixed face amount and fixed premium policy, this could be the policy of choice.

Single Premium Whole Life Insurance

Single premium whole life insurance frequently is structured as an interest-sensitive whole life contract allowing only one premium. As we have indicated, whole life insurance is a fixed premium, fixed face amount contract. Single premium whole life insurance is a fixed premium, fixed face amount policy with but one premium allowed. The policy is designed to accept at issue the maximum premium allowable, relative to its face amount, under the income tax regulation laid out in Section 7702 of the Internal Revenue Code. In other words, the investment in the policy is maximized. Since the investment is maximized, the net amount at risk is minimized. Net amount at risk may be defined as that amount that must be paid by the insurance company in the event of the death of the insured that is strictly insurance company money and not a return of the policyowner's investment or account value.

Reducing the amount at risk to a minimum also reduces mortality charges to a minimum. Since the policy will accept only one premium, expenses are minimized. The underlying investment, therefore, has as little of its return as possible allocated to mortality and expense charges. By maximizing investment and minimizing life insurance, investors took advantage of the fact that the investment within the insurance policy could earn without current taxation and could be recovered via policy loan without taxation. Uncle Sam changed this situation as of June 21, 1988. The insurance companies aggressively designed these single premium policies in order to attract investment dollars. They promised consumers a net rate of return on the investment capital after all expenses and mortality charges were paid. In other words, the insurance company would take your money on a single premium policy investment and promise you, for example, 8%. The insurance company had determined that it could lend that same money out at possibly 9%. The spread between what they were paying you, 8%, and what was being paid to them, 9%, would have to cover all mortality and expense charges and still provide some profit for the insurance company.

Since the net rates of return without current taxation were so competitive with other alternative investments, single premium life attracted quite a bit of consumer attention. It was purchased even by those who had no interest in the life insurance element. Consumers liked the fact that within the policy they could earn compound interest without current taxation. They also could borrow those untaxed earnings and spend that money without paying current taxes on what they had borrowed. You probably could borrow the money from your policy at an interest rate of 6% and at the same time the insurance company would credit your policy on the amount you had borrowed with an identical 6%. Thus a policyowner could borrow and enjoy tax-free income, within limits, for potentially substantial periods of time with little or no effective cost. Despite the big income tax trap in this if you terminate the policy in any way other than by dying, that all the deferred past taxes must be paid—and despite the fact that not many policyowners took advantage of the loan feature, it was viewed with disfavor by our legislators. The ability to borrow without triggering current taxation on gains within a single premium life insurance policy was terminated, effective for policies issued after June 20, 1988. Thereafter, any monies borrowed from single premium life policies or modified endowments (a whole new class of life insurance policies) would trigger current taxation to the extent of any gains in the policy. The borrowing policyowner would also be subject to penalty taxes of 10% of the amount included in gross income if that policyowner was less than 59 ½ years of age. Exceptions to the penalty tax are made in the event of an individual's disability or if there is annuitization of the policy proceeds.

You also can maximize premium payments into other types of policies, such as universal life, universal variable life and single premium variable life. Universal variable and universal life policies of course, are not single-premium contracts. However, you can maximize your investment into the policy in a single premium, which means that you have paid as much as the law will allow you to pay into that policy at that particular time. It is entirely possible that in the future additional premiums may be paid into such policies and the policies will still remain within the IRC 7702 restrictions on how much investment a policy can accept and still remain a life insurance policy.

Since June 21, 1988, single premium and investment oriented policies, called modified endowments, have lost appeal as retirement vehicles and sources of ready cash as a result of the change in the law. If the policyowner takes money from such contracts, he must accept the fact that there will be immediate income taxation to the extent of gain and, if the policyowner is under age 59 ½, there also will be a 10% penalty of the amount included in gross income.

The single premium policy is still an advantageous vehicle for an insured's beneficiaries. It still efficiently transfers wealth that has enjoyed tax-free compounding for a substantial period of time to the beneficiaries without any income tax liabilities. All life insurance proceeds payable at death are excluded from income taxation under section 101 of the Internal Revenue Code.

Summary

Figure 8–2 summarizes the life insurance marketplace in a one-page matrix. The basic, inevitable, components of a life insurance policy are the mortality and expense charges. As a result of paying these charges to an insurance company, the insurance company will pool your resources with those of other policyowners and will agree to pay a death benefit to your beneficiaries. The forms of life insurance vary according to how you pay these mortality and expense charges. The first generic form of life insurance is term insurance in which you pay just enough to cover the mortality and expense charges. All other forms of life insurance are policies that require mortality and expense charges plus an extra amount for investment purposes. Part, all, or more than your total investment return will be used to cover mortality and expense charges as required by the net amount at risk (amount of insurance company money that would be paid to the beneficiary in the event of the insured's death). The four generic forms of these term "plus" investment policies are whole life, variable life, universal life and universal variable life.

The next issue to address is how to manage these life insurance policies and what investment opportunities life insurance offers to you, the policyowner.

Figure 8–4
Life Insurance Contract Suitability and Selection Questionnaire

1. The Life Insurance Product Analyzer in Figure 8–2 summarizes the variations in life insurance based upon six ways of paying for and investing in life insurance. After going over the matrix, complete the following indicating your preferences:
    Put a check mark under the word that best describes your initial reaction to the type of policy named.

	Highly Prefer	Prefer	Satis-factory	Accept-able	Unsatis-factory
Non-guaranteed Term	____	____	____	____	____
Yearly Renewable and Convertible Term	____	____	____	____	____
Whole Life	____	____	____	____	____
Universal Life	____	____	____	____	____
Variable Life	____	____	____	____	____
Universal/Variable Life	____	____	____	____	____

2. I wish to put enough money into a life insurance policy to buy the life insurance protection only—no investment.
    True   False

3. At this time, I am not able to consider investing with an insurance company.
    True   False

4. I prefer not to invest with a life insurance company.
    True   False

5. The term policy need not be renewable or convertible as long as it provides uninterrupted life insurance for at least _____ years.
    True   False

6. I want the term policy to contain renewability and convertibility features.
    True   False

7. I would prefer to invest capital with an insurance company and have the charges for expenses and term insurance (mortality costs) deducted from my investment account earnings (pre-tax).
    True   False

8. I prefer the whole life policy which invests in the long-term bond and mortgage portfolio of the life insurance company.

True   False

9. I prefer the whole life arrangement of paying for life insurance for all of the following reasons.

Check the reasons for your preference in the list below:

_____ Not applicable.

_____ I like long-term bond and mortgage investments for life insurance.

_____ I wish to use a very conservative investment account within my policy.

_____ I desire low volatility.

_____ I prefer a fixed, contractually guaranteed premium.

_____ I desire a relatively high degree of assurance that my payments into the policy may be eliminated, e.g., a "short pay" policy with a seven- to twelve-year time frame, with a high degree of confidence that premiums will not have to be paid after that time.

_____ I prefer a low management type of policy.

_____ I do not want premium, face amount or investment flexibility.

_____ Other.

_____

_____

_____

10. I prefer the Universal Life arrangement of paying for life insurance for all of the following reasons.

Check the reasons for your preference in the list below:

_____ Not applicable.

_____ I prefer having the insurance company specify each year the interest I will earn on the capital invested within my policy as determined by market conditions and at the company's discretion.

_____ The guaranteed interest account is sufficient for my life insurance investment purposes. I do not and will not want or need any other investment alternatives in the future.

_____ I like being able to see exactly what my investment is earning and the exact charges being made against my policy.

_____ I like the flexibility of being able to adjust the face amount of the policy.

_____ I like the flexibilty of being able to vary my premium payments into the policy.

_____ I want face amount and premium flexibility but not investment flexibility.

_____ Other

_____

_____

_____

11. I prefer the variable whole life arrangement of paying for life insurance for all the following reasons.

Check your reasons for your preference in the list below:

_____ Not applicable.

_____ I like the security of knowing I only need to pay a fixed annual premium to maintain my policy regardless of what happens to my policy investments, mortality costs or expenses.

_____ I like the fixed premium arrangement.

_____ I like having the ability to invest in a variety of investment accounts and being able to reposition these investments.

_____ I do not want premium or face amount flexibility, just investment flexibility.

_____ I like the guarantee that my death benefit will never go below the original face amount of the policy.

_____ Other

_____

_____

_____

12. I prefer the Universal/Variable arrangement of paying for life insurance for all the following reasons.

Check your reasons for your preference in the list below:

_____ Not applicable.

_____ I desire the flexibility this policy offers with regard to face amount, premium payments into the policy and the investment alternatives available in the policy.

_____ I welcome the opportunity to exercise management control over premium, face amount and investments in this policy and to enjoy the living benefits that it offers to enhance my family's/company's security. I am aware of the responsibility that is inherent in such flexibility.

_____ I want to have the opportunity to use the family of mutual funds within a policy to accumulate for family investment objectives without creating income tax liabilities.

_____ I like the idea of having access to a family of mutual funds sheltered from current taxation.

_____ I prefer to retain premium flexibility, face amount flexibility and investment flexibility.

_____ Other

_____

_____

_____

Review your answers to these questions. They have been designed to make you look at the generic forms of life insurance and to help you determine which you currently prefer.

If your choice is yearly renewable and convertible term life insurance, make sure that you have also determined your preference among the investment forms of life insurance and that the company from whom you are buying term life insurance also has the type of investment-oriented policy you may wish to convert to in the future.

NINE

MANAGING YOUR LIFE INSURANCE

You can and should manage your life insurance. You cannot afford to ignore the substantial accumulation of wealth that exists in these policies as a result of premiums paid and the earnings on investments within the policy. Yet most of you still do just that. It is no longer justified or necessary. You will find today's new life insurance policies are much easier to understand and manage.

The first level of management is the amount of the policy's death benefit. In Chapter 7, we tried to assist you in determining a total face amount of life insurance that would be appropriate for you. You may obtain additional assistance in making this determination from a life insurance salesperson, an accountant, an attorney, a bank trust officer or a financial planner. However, *you* are the final decision maker. Your sense of values will determine an appropriate amount for the beneficiaries that you are seeking to protect. Once the face amount decision has been made, the next decision will be how much should you pay into a life insurance policy.

Whole Life and Variable Life

If you have chosen a whole life or a variable whole life policy, the insurance company will dictate the amount of premium to be paid each year based upon the face amount, the number of years that you have agreed to continue to pay a premium, your age, sex, smoking habits, and your health. These are fixed premium policies. You may elect to pay for the policy with a single premium, with premiums payable each year for the rest of your life, or somewhere between these two extremes. We refer to these as fixed premium, fixed face amount policies because your decisions regarding face amount and billed premium level are made when the policy is applied for and are not altered by the insurance company thereafter. With these policies, you must apply and qualify for a new policy if you want more life insurance, rather than simply adding additional coverage to the existing contract.

In a whole life contract your investment is fixed also. It is stipulated to be the long-term general account or the short-term general account (interest sensitive whole life) of the insurance company from which you have purchased the policy. There are no future choices that may be made. If you wanted to direct the capital in that policy to some alternative investment, your only choice would be to borrow or withdraw funds from that policy and put them to work outside of the contract.

With variable whole life insurance, your level of premium payment and face amount is fixed as of the application date, but the funds may be invested in any of the accounts the insurance company makes available to you within the policy. Thus, the variable contract comes with a fixed premium and face amount but with a variable investment vehicle, whereas whole life has a fixed face amount, premium and investment vehicle.

Adjustable Premium Policies

In an effort to increase premium payment flexibility within whole life insurance policies, some insurance companies have issued what they refer to as adjustable policies. The adjustable feature gives you management control over the premium level of the policy when you submit a *written* request to the insurance company to adjust the current premium payment to an alternative level of premium payment. In effect, the premium payment period is shortened if you ask for an increase in premium or lengthened if you wish to reduce the premium. To go to the lowest allowable premium level normally turns the policy into a 10-year term contract because insufficient premium is being paid into the policy to keep it in force for the rest of the insured's life. These policies are less flexible than the unwritten policies that require no written requests in advance. These policies do not demand as sophisticated a computer system as universal policies.

Term Insurance

Term life insurance probably requires the least amount of management on the part of the policyowner. The policyowner stipulates face amount, submits to a physical examination and questions regarding occupation, avocations, health habits, smoking, and so on. Then, based upon the insurance company's determination of the risk involved, the policyowner is asked to pay a stipulated premium for a stipulated time. In the case of annual renewable and convertible term insurance, the annual premium is sufficient to cover the mortality and expenses required by the policy for one year. As the Product Analyzer in Figure 8–1 shows, there are varying types of term insurance. The short-term objective of those who buy term insurance is to pay the least possible amount of cash out-of-pocket for such protection. Figure 9–1 illustrates some term insurance costs based upon rates for a male non-smoker purchasing a $250,000 face amount policy. It shows the approximate amount you would pay on a per thousand dollar basis into such policies. These rates are for planning purposes only since life insurance rates change rapidly and can vary significantly based upon your health and the amount of insurance you choose to purchase. Insurance companies frequently give discounts to purchasers of larger policies which means that the per thousand cost comes down at higher levels of policy face amount.

In Chapter 7, we decided that once the need for life insurance was identified, the first order of business was to put a life insurance policy in force. Take your beneficiaries off the hook by putting the insurance company on the hook. Yearly renewable and convertible term insurance is the most expeditious way of doing this with the least amount of commitment on your part. Use renewable and convertible term insurance and make sure that you understand the privileges granted you within the contract for the premium you pay. Do they allow you to change your term insurance policy to any of the other varieties of life insurance—is it convertible? Does the particular company from whom you are buying the term policy have a variety of life insurance types to which you may wish to convert? In most cases, when you convert your term policy into another type of contract, you will get credit for the premium you have paid for the term insurance in the year of conversion. As a result, you have nothing to lose by putting the term policy in force immediately, and making the management decisions concerning the long-term financing of that policy at a more leisurely pace.

Figure 9–1 shows representative term rates for four different products: 1) a very limited non-convertible, non-renewable three year term product, 2) a low-load yearly renewable term product, 3) a commercial insurance company term rate and 4) the term rates within a universal or universal variable policy. Column 5) shows the maximum rates an insurer can charge. These are the 1980 Commisioners Standard Ordinary Mortality Table Rates (1980 CSO).

As a life insurance buyer and policyowner, your second management decision is basically which of the term rates

Figure 9–1
Representative Term Insurance Rates
Male non-smoker rates, $250,000 face amount
Cost per year per $1,000

AGE	(1)	(2)	(3)	(4)	(5)
25	.49	.88	1.07	1.14	1.77
30	.49	.88	1.14	1.14	1.73
35	.49	.92	1.20	1.24	2.11
40	.52	1.13	1.34	1.43	3.02
45	.77	1.72	1.98	2.09	4.55
50	1.20	3.16	3.16	3.52	6.71
55	1.75	4.37	4.31	5.01	10.47
60	2.68	6.63	7.66	8.43	16.08
65	4.27	12.17	12.08	14.34	25.42
70	5.90	N/A	25.92	23.25	39.51
75	14.72	N/A	55.39	41.79	64.19

1) Non-Guaranteed Term—3 year coverage limit

2) United Services Automobile Association (USAA) direct purchase Annual Renewable Term—No Commission Product—Add $30 per year policy fee

3) Commercial Insurance Company Term Rates (1989)— Add $30 per year policy fee

4) Mortality/Term Insurance charges inside a Universal or Universal/Variable Life Insurance Policy

5) Maximum Mortality Charges—1980 Commissioners Standard Ordinary Mortality Table

shown in Figure 9–1 should you pay . . . and how do you wish to pay them?

Non-Guaranteed Term

If you elect column number one in Figure 9–1, the non-guaranteed term life insurance policy, make sure that the period of time for which the protection is offered is identical to the period of time for which you want and need the life insurance coverage. Although this is the lowest cost term insurance understand that the risk that you face with this type of policy is that you lose control over this policy at the end of the period of time for which you bought coverage. Your insurance objectives and your health may have changed by that time. The continuation of that policy might be very valuable for you, but you would not be able to continue it. Murphy's Law tends to come into play in such situations. It is referred to as "cheap" term in the product analyzer because you do not control it, the insurance company does.

Low-Load Term

It is possible to purchase life insurance without going through a commissioned agent. In some eastern states, such as New York, you may buy life insurance from the bank. You may also go to an insurance company in San Antonio, Texas called United Services Automobile Association (USAA) and purchase insurance directly over the phone without the involvement of a commissioned agent. Column number two in Figure 9–1 gives some representative rates for USAA policies for a male non-smoker at the $250,000 face amount level. With any insurance company, you may be able to get lower rates than are shown in this column by purchasing higher face amount policies.

Can you accomplish your purchase without the assistance of an agent? USAA life allows you to convert this policy to other forms of life insurance available from USAA Life. Do they have the alternative policies that you may want? These are important questions that should affect your purchase decision.

A word about "no-load" insurance is in order. First, in its pure form, it does not exist. An insurance company may or may not pay commissioned salespeople, or they may pay them a little ("low-load"), but every insurance company does have marketing costs and purchasers pay these costs. A wise purchaser determines exactly how much is saved by buying a product touted as "no-load" or "low-load." There is no such thing as a no-load plumber, doctor, dentist, accountant or store owner. You can't buy no-load cars, suits, food, medicines or anything else. You are not in a no-load business or your family would not be eating, let alone buying life insurance. Consumers pay people to help them with their life insurance purchases. The key is not "to pay or not to pay"; the key is to receive full value for what you are paying. If you do reward an agent with your business, make sure that you select carefully and that the agent deserves your business and puts your best interests first.

The third column in Figure 9–1 shows representative rates for term insurance available from commercial life insurance companies which pay commissions to agents. You would purchase this type of policy if it is convenient and if the assistance and advice from the agent who will earn the commissions will be of value to you. The agent should provide sufficient "value added" to the policy to make any additional amounts you may pay for the policy worthwhile. You should evaluate the agent's ability to do so based on recommendations from your other financial advisers and the individual agent's background, education and activities. Above all, you should sense in the agent a personal concern for your well-being. Dismiss that agent if you ever sense that commission earnings are more important than your personal objectives. There are too many good insurance sales representatives available for you to do business with one who isn't attentive and professional.

When shopping for term insurance remember that the mortality costs, which comprise the major portion of your payments into these policies (the balance being expenses), go up every year as you get older. The insurers issue policies in different ways to pass this inevitably increasing cost on to you at varying rates. They may raise the premium every year or average it over a given span of years. They may keep the cost constant and take away some of your insurance protection, as in decreasing term insurance, frequently referred to as mortgage insurance. Unfortunately, "lowballing" is used too frequently in the industry. A company may promise low rates in a marketing letter, but after you buy you may find that rates increase rapidly in the future.

Be careful of the quote services that promise to find you low rates. If they are licensed insurance sales organizations, they earn a commission if you buy from them so they do not particularly care whether all facets of a policy fit your needs. Indeed it is unlikely they will know or ask about your needs—they sell you whatever you perceive as the cheapest policy. A quick sale is a profitable one for them.

If the company is a fee-only quote provider their only real interest is collecting the fee. Charging fifty dollars to mail out computer printouts is profitable business for them but possibly a waste of money for you.

In most cases you can get the same information plus explanations and assistance from your life insurance professional. Save your $50, and buy or not buy at your discretion. Don't be afraid of insurance salespeople! Fire the bad ones . . . buy from those who put your needs first and serve you well.

In your term policy check for guaranteed renewability that allows you to keep the policy in force for as long as you want. Compare forecasted renewal rates for the duration during which you plan on continuing the policy. Avoid "reentry" term policies that give you favorable rates only if you can pass another medical examination. Do not be too concerned about the level of the guaranteed maximum term premiums the insurance company can charge you. These rates are the company's rates as filed with state regulators of insurance. Competition in the field will never allow the rates to go exceptionally high unless some catastrophic epidemic drives all insurance companies' rates up. The factors that force term rates up will affect the whole industry, so that if rates *do* go to the maximums, most, if not all, companies will have to do the same.

Term Insurance Costs

Every life insurance policy includes a charge to policyowners for mortality costs and expenses. Some policies stipulate exactly how much you have been charged each year for these elements, and some do not. The policies that itemize all costs and benefits within the contract are the straight term policies and the universal and universal-variable life policies. The rates in column number four of Figure 9–1 are the mortality or term insurance rates charged by one commercial insurance company within their universal and universal/variable life insurance policies.

After-Tax Term

When choosing a term policy from columns one, two or three of Figure 9–1, you are electing to pay a term premium for a straight term insurance policy based upon the death benefit offered. For any of these contracts you will be paying for the policy with your "after-tax earnings." You will have to earn enough money to pay income tax on the earnings and have enough left over to pay premiums to the insurance company. For example, if you are a male, age 45 and a non-smoker, you could buy $250,000 worth of life insurance from USAA life at the rate of $1.72 per thousand (as quoted in Figure 9–1). Your premium for the $250,000 worth of insurance would be approximately $430.00 (250 × $1.72). In order for you to have $430 to send to the insurance company, you would have to earn $614.00 [$430.00 divided by one minus your marginal tax bracket (1-30%), or $430 divided by .70]. Having earned $614, you would send 30% of that to Uncle Sam in taxes—$184— and you would have $430 left to send to the insurance company. You had to earn $614 in order to have $430 left, after taxes, to pay for your life insurance. That is buying life insurance with after-tax earnings: in order to pay $1.72 per thousand, you must earn $2.46 per $1,000.

Pre-Tax Term or Minimizing Term Costs by Cutting Out Uncle Sam

Why would you want to pay $2.09 per thousand, the cost per thousand indicated in column number four of Figure 9–1, as the term cost in a universal or universal/variable life policy, rather than the $1.72 per thousand to USAA used in the above example? The reason is that the $2.09 may be paid with pre-tax earnings on your investment within the contract. You only have to earn $2.09 to pay the insurance company $2.09, versus the $2.46 you would have to earn to pay $1.72 for the straight term policy—a savings of 37 cents per $1,000. This represents a savings of 15%! The question is: "Do you have after-tax capital available to reposition into an insurance policy in order to enjoy tax-free earnings to pay term premiums?"

Funding Levels in Universal and Universal/Variable Policies

Once the decision has been made to buy life insurance with pre-tax dollars earned on an investment account, the decisions of *how much* to invest, and *where* to invest, remain. If you have decided on conventional whole life that invests in long-term bonds and mortgages, or the interest-sensitive variety which invests in short-term money market types of investments, both the "amount to invest" decision and the "where to invest" decisions have been made. The company tells you how much to pay based upon the face amount and the type of policy in which you invest. There is little flexibility of premium payment after that. Similarly, with variable whole life, you agree at contract inception to a set premium and face amount, but retain management control and flexibility over where the money is to be invested in the contract.

On the other hand, funding level decisions with universal life are important not only on the day you decide on a specific face amount of life insurance and put the policy in force, but continue to be an important decision throughout the life of the contract. The ability to vary premium payments gives the

Figure 9–2
Funding Levels in Universal and Universal/Variable Policies

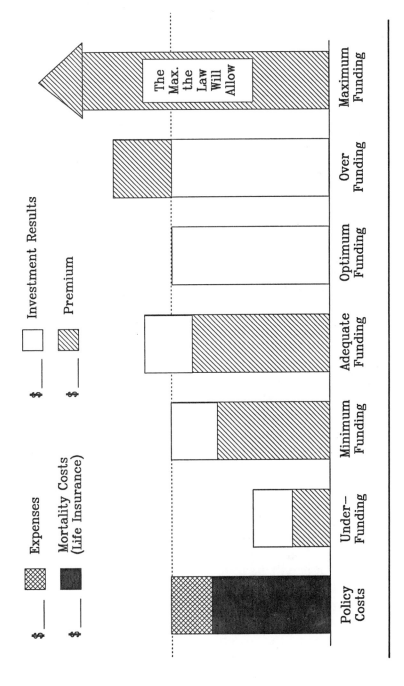

Figure 9–3
Optimum Funding

Current Investment
Results
                        "Equal"
                                    Expenses Plus
                                    Mortality Charges

---

policyowner important investment opportunities. To take advantage of this opportunity it may help you to think of your funding strategy as one of the following: under-funding, minimum funding, adequate funding, optimum funding, over-funding or maximum funding. A description of each strategy follows.

Optimum Funding Level

We have determined that the primary objective of the life insurance policy is to provide life insurance protection in the amount you deem necessary. You want to pay for this insurance in the most efficient way possible. Optimum funding level in a life insurance policy is the point at which the amount of policyowner capital invested inside the policy will earn enough non-taxable return in the year in question to pay all of the mortality and expense charges within the policy in that year. Such a strategy assures that you will be paying for your life insurance with the pre-tax earnings on the after-tax capital you have invested in your insurance policy. As long as the mortality and expense charges are fair, adequate and competitive, you will have accomplished your primary objective of providing life insurance coverage at the least possible cost by paying that cost with earnings not subject to income tax.

To determine optimum funding level, you need to know the amount of the expenses and the mortality charges to be charged within your policy for the year. This information is readily available in universal and universal/variable policies. Whole life and variable whole life policies, however, do not divulge the amount of these costs. Universal policies provide a way for *you* to manage your investment based upon costs that exist in all policies whether such costs are divulged or not. The optimum funding level is determined by dividing the amount of the expenses and mortality charges for the year, by the return expected or guaranteed for that year. If your mortality and expenses are to be $400 this year and your return is 8%, then you will need $5,000 in your policy to reach optimum funding level. That is, $5,000 earning 8% will generate $400 of pre-tax interest, which is sufficient to cover $400 worth of expenses and mortality charges.

Recall the example of a 45-year old buying a $250,000 straight term insurance policy at an annual premium of $430 in the first year. To generate the $430 after taxes, he had to earn $614 [$430 divided by (1 minus his marginal tax bracket)]. Alternatively, he could have elected to pay $2.09 per thousand (column four, Figure 9–1) inside a universal variable policy, a premium of $523. Also, he found $48 in expenses being charged on that policy each year, bringing the total cost for mortality and expenses in the universal/variable policy to $571 for year one. This policyowner has the option of investing enough after-tax capital in the policy so that the untaxed earnings would be sufficient to pay the $571. The policyowner would thus save $43 ($614 minus $571) in the year in question if the tax-free return on $7,138 of capital ($571 divided by 8%) in the policy is competitive with alternative investment opportunities.

Alternatively, if the same $7,138 was invested elsewhere, it would have to earn 8.6% to guarantee the $614 of taxable earnings required to service a $430 straight term premium. If the policyowner can obtain either an 8% tax-free return outside of the policy, or almost a 8.6% taxable return, the decision to buy straight term or to pay for term insurance inside of a universal or universal/variable becomes a toss up. However, the returns offered within these policies typically are very competitive, offer generally lower risks and offer future term rates that are often lower than those available elsewhere.

The next decision is to determine where to invest the capital among the choices offered within the policy. The uni-

---

Figure 9–4
Adequate Funding

Current Premium
Plus
Investment Results

"Exceed"

Expenses Plus
Mortality Charges

---

versal life policy will offer only one choice, guaranteed interest, whereas the universal/variable will offer multiple choices. The first investment objective within the policy would be to seek an investment account that would produce the type of investment results that are needed to service the policy's expense and mortality charges. The need is for monthly income to cover monthly costs. An investment vehicle that is appropriate to serve that particular need would be the guaranteed principal, guaranteed interest account, a money market account or some other account that generates dependable monthly income. A universal/variable policy normally will offer at least one account suitable for paying the mortality and expense charges in addition to other accounts that can be used for your other investment objectives.

Adequate Funding

We have defined optimum funding as a strategy whereby investment proceeds in the policy generate enough investment return to pay all mortality and expense charges incurred in the policy in the year in question. Adequate funding level is for those who do not have, or do not wish to invest sufficient capital within a policy to reach optimum funding level immediately. We can define adequate funding in terms of optimum funding by saying that it is a level of payments designed to allow you to arrive at optimum funding at some particular point in time. Policyowners who know where they are going and when they are going to get there are "adequately" fund-

Figure 9–5
Under Funding

Current Premium
Plus
Investment Results

"Is Less Than"

Expenses Plus
Mortality Charges

---

ing their policy. Adequate funding level is a funding level that will get a policyowner to optimum funding level over a policyowner selected period of time. In the example above, approximately $6,000 in capital is needed to reach optimum funding. If that particular policyowner doesn't have $6,000 to put into the policy immediately, but wants to accumulate that capital, he sets up a funding level strategy to get to optimum funding level. He may decide on an investment of $100 per month, $1,200 a year. At this rate of funding he can reasonably expect, based upon projected mortality costs, expenses, and interest earnings, that he will arrive at optimum funding in approximately five years. Periodically, at least yearly, he can check the policy to see how it is progressing, and adjust the funding level to current situations and objectives.

Under-funding

Under-funding of universal and universal/variable life policies occurs when the mortality and expense charges exceed the combined total of the investment earnings in the policy and the current year's payment into the policy. For example, when you examine your universal or universal/variable life policy, you find that expenses incurred for the year were $50 and mortality costs were $450, totalling $500 in costs for that particular year. Upon further examination, you find that interest earnings in your policy amounted to only $100 and, upon inspecting your checkbook, you find that you have only paid $100 into the policy during the year. Your contribution and the interest earnings totaled $200, whereas expenses totaled $500. In order to cover the $500 due in expenses, the policy was forced to take a $300 bite out of principal—the capital previously accumulated in the policy. At the end of the year, you will find $300 less capital in the policy than you had when you began the year. If you ignore this process you will find in the coming year that you will have still less capital to earn interest. If you don't increase your contributions, you'll find at the end of that year another decrease in capital that will exceed the decrease of the previous year. The situation gets worse as the mortality charges in the policy increase as you get older. The expense charges also may be increased to some contractual maximum, and the interest earnings in the policy could be decreased because of changes in the prevailing level of interest rates. If all four events occur at the same time (capital down, interest rates down, expenses up, mortality costs up), your policy would consume its principal at an even more rapid pace. As the capital base in your policy approaches depletion, the insurance company will let you know that unless you start making payments into that contract, it will terminate. Under-funded policies eat up principal within the contract at an ever-increasing rate—don't let this happen to you!

When universal life policies first appeared in 1979 and 1980, interest rates were high. Funding levels were chosen during those periods assuming that those inordinately high interest rates were going to stay as high as they were at the time. Many of these policies are under-funded and indeed many of them have actually been involuntarily terminated. Angry policyowners do not understand why their policies are being terminated. That has resulted in consumer complaints to state insurance commissioners.

In many cases, even insurance salespeople who were selling these policies were not sure what they were selling. In competitive situations, an agent could sell you the same amount of coverage at a "cheaper" rate. This smaller premium represented a lower investment and lower investment returns. Lower investment returns meant lower tax-free interest and thus a less efficient policy. Under-funding is the poorest of

---

Figure 9–6
Minimum Funding

Current Premium
Plus
Investment Results

     "Is Equal To"

          Expenses Plus
          Mortality Charges

---

strategies in a universal or universal/variable life policy. It is wiser to buy a yearly renewable and convertible term policy with after-tax dollars. Minimum funding should be the lowest funding level into a universal or universal/variable policy.

Minimum Funding Level

The minimum funding level for these types of policies should be the level at which the interest earnings in the policy and the policyowner's contribution to the policy are no less than the amount of the mortality and expense charges in the policy in that particular year. Such a funding level will assure that the capital accumulated within your contract will stay at a constant level for the year and not be depleted by policy costs. It's an advantage to own a policy in which you can adjust the premium level back to that of a straight term policy during

---

Figure 9–7
Over–Funding

Current Investment
Results

     "Exceed"

          Expenses Plus
          Mortality Charges

---

those times when you do not have extra money to invest in the policy but try hard not to pay so little in that your policy is forced to deplete its capital.

Over–Funding

If you have reached the optimum funding level and policy earnings are sufficient to cover all policy expenses, why would you choose to invest even more capital? We will assume that you have purchased a universal/variable life policy and start out in a strategy of adequate funding. This strategy may be interspersed periodically in years of stress with years of minimum funding. One day you attain optimum funding— the point at which expenses and mortality charges are entirely covered by policy earnings. If you have been utilizing the guaranteed-principal, guaranteed-interest account to hold the monies that represent the optimum funding level as we have suggested, you still have the family of mutual funds available for your use. These differ from commercially available mutual funds by the fact that earnings, capital gains, dividends and interest earnings within these mutual funds create no current income tax liability. You have enjoyed tax-free compounding in your IRA's and qualified retirement plans, and now this is available to you within your life insurance policy as well.

Many of you participate in successful mutual funds and use them appropriately to build family wealth. Such mutual funds outside of the life insurance policy require the payment of taxes each year on any earnings and capital gains. In 1989, for example, you probably will be required to send to Uncle Sam almost one-third of realized capital gains, dividends and interest earnings in any mutual fund that is subject to current taxation. During the year, if you decide to sell one of your mutual funds and reinvest the money from that sale in a different mutual fund, the transaction will result in current taxation on the capital gains realized. The sale of the investment in one fund of a family of funds and the repositioning of those assets into another of that family's mutual funds will cause taxation on any capital gains realized from the sale.

Figure 9–8
Maximum Funding

Current Premium
                    "Equal"
                              The Maximum
                              the Law
                              Will Allow

Over-funding is a strategy available to you if you own a universal/variable life insurance policy. Funds may be invested using this strategy and you will not share your gains with Uncle Sam. The gains will be reinvested intact into the funds and taxation will be deferred until some future point in time or if the policy pays off as a death benefit, the gains will escape income tax entirely.

If you own a universal/variable policy, taxable mutual funds are obsolete for you until that policy has reached its maximum funding level.

Maximum Funding

Maximum funding level is based upon the policy death benefit, which dictates the point at which no additional funds can be added to the policy based upon the controlling income tax provisions in Internal Revenue Code Section 7702. According to the tax code, funding above this level causes the policy to cease to be a life insurance policy, resulting in immediate taxation of all deferred earnings. Your insurance company should not accept money that would cause your policy to go above maximum funding.

To determine if an over-funding strategy would be advantageous for you, you must first determine exactly what additional expenses, if any, will be incurred when you send in additional investment dollars. The first thing you will find is that these additional investment dollars will be diminished by state premium taxes. State premium taxes are charged by your

Figure 9–9
State Premium Taxes as of March 9, 1988
Life Insurance
(State of Residences of Insured)

State	Tax Rate %	State	Tax Rate %	State	Tax Rate %
Alabama	4	Kentucky	2.5	Ohio	2.5
Alaska	2.7	Louisiana	3.25	Oklahoma	4
Arizona	1.7	Maine	2	Oregon	2.25
Arkansas	2.5	Maryland	2	Pennsylvania	2
California	2.35	Massachusetts	2	Puerto Rico	4
Colorado	2.25	Michigan	2	Rhode Island	2
Connecticut	2	Minnesota	2	South Carolina	.75
Delaware	2	Mississippi	3	South Dakota	2.5
D.C.	2	Missouri	2	Tennessee	2
Florida	2	Montana	2.75	Texas	3
Georgia	2.25	Nebraska	1	Utah	2.25
Guam	1	Nevada	2.5	Vermont	2
Hawaii	3.197	New Hampshire	2	Virginia	2.25
Idaho	3.663	New Jersey	2	Virgin Islands	4
Illinois	2	New Mexico	3	Washington	2
Indiana	2	New York	3	West Virginia	3
Iowa	2	North Carolina	1.75	Wisconsin	2
Kansas	2	North Dakota	2	Wyoming	2.5

Figure 9–9 (continued)
Annuity State Premium Tax Rates

State	Non-Qualified	Qualified Including IRAs
Alabama	1.00%	1.00%
California	2.35	0.50
Kansas	2.00	None
Kentucky	2.00	2.00
Maine	2.00	None
Mississippi	2.00	None
Nevada	3.00	None
North Carolina	1.75	None
Puerto Rico	1.00	1.00
South Dakota	1.25	None
Virgin Islands	2.00	2.00
Washington, D.C.	2.00	2.00
West Virginia	1.00	1.00
Wyoming	1.00	None

States omitted have *no* state premium tax deducted.

state of residence on every premium that is paid into a life insurance policy. The additional investment we are discussing is considered a premium payment under the state regulations.

Figure 9–9 lists the state premium taxes as charged by the individual states. You may be one of the fortunate people who live in the State of New York and find that only eight-tenths of one percent of your investments will go to state premium taxes. In this case, a $100 premium would incur only an eighty-cent tax. If the insurance company makes no additional charges against your $100 investment, you will find $99.20 going to work for you in your accumulation account. In this case, this charge will probably be lower than most low-load mutual funds. On the other hand, residents of Alabama, Oklahoma, Puerto Rico or the Virgin Islands have a state premium tax of 4 percent. This means an investment into the mutual fund of $100 is going to be diminished by $4—only $96 will be invested and go to work for you. In either case, it is likely that you can find investments within your life insurance policy advantageous to you because of the income tax savings involved and the tax-free compounding you will enjoy. Determine these costs before you buy a policy. Beware of percentage charges against premium payments in excess of state premium charges,—a ploy sometimes used by supposed "no-load" or "low-load" insurance companies.

One of the advantages the universal/variable product has over the straight universal product is that the universal/variable product is a registered product, subject to the regulations under the Investment Acts of 1938, 1939, and 1940. These products must provide a prospectus providing total disclosure and defining certain limitations on expenses. This prospectus will be invaluable to you in determining the charges that you will incur within your policy and also the investment results on the various investment alternatives. Typically, these reports will compare their investments to some readily available baseline. The prospectus and annual policy reports will describe the funds, stating their objectives and investment philosophies. Your objective in selecting such a policy is to find one with a family of funds in which the investment manager's objectives are in concert with your own, one that has acceptable investment risks and whose long-term return will be satisfactory to you. These funds levy charges for management, which will be taken from the fund's total return, just as in all mutual funds. Normally the reports you get will be based upon a net return after these expenses. Although it may seem that low fund management expenses would result in a higher net return to you, remember that you cannot skimp on management fees and buy good managers. The value you receive for the fees that you pay is substantially more important than low fees.

In summary, if you have quality mutual funds within your life insurance policy which are comparable in performance and expenses to the field of taxable mutual funds, use them to the maximum extent possible prior to using taxable mutual funds.

Figure 9–10
Income Tax Benefits of a Life Insurance Contract

1. Death benefits from a life insurance contract are excluded from the beneficiary's income. Death benefits include net amount at risk and policyowner equity within the contract, plus earnings.

2. The annual increase in value (inside buildup) is not subject to current taxation and escapes taxation entirely at death.

3. The income tax basis of your policy includes amounts expended for life insurance and expenses.

4. In life insurance policies other than "modified endowment" contracts, withdrawals up to policyowner basis are taxed first in, first out, thus without income tax liability. Policy loans are not currently taxable except in "modified endowment" policies.

The Four Income Tax Benefits of Life Insurance

One: Death Benefits —Income Tax-free

The primary advantage of life insurance is that if, when the life insurance "hat" is passed, you contribute a small sum and subsequently die, the whole hat will be given to your beneficiaries. This is good not only for beneficiaries but also for society, since these beneficiaries then do not become economically dependent upon society. The death benefits of life insurance policies have therefore been exempted from income taxation. It doesn't matter whether the death benefit comes from "net amount at risk," from the policyowner's investment in the contract, or from the positive investment results—it is all tax-free income under Section 101 of the Internal Revenue Code. This, the first income tax benefit of life insurance, is enjoyed by all life insurance policies. However, there are many ways to mismanage your policy with the result that the death benefit becomes taxable, such as selling your policy to another for valuable consideration; don't make any such changes without considering them carefully with your income tax advisors.

Two: Current Earnings and Gains Not Currently Taxed

The second advantage of life insurance is that during the insured's lifetime, and while the policy is still in force, all interest earned, dividends earned and/or capital gains realized on the policy investments are not subject to current income tax. The taxation is deferred until the gains are taken from the policy by the policyowner. All investment life insurance policies enjoy tax-deferral on this "inside build-up" and a possibility of total tax-exemption on investment returns within the contract, which occurs when the proceeds are disbursed as death benefits.

Three: Policy Tax Basis Includes Amounts Paid for Life Insurance and Expenses

The third income tax benefit of life insurance containing investment capital is that the amount of money you recover tax-free when you surrender your policy includes all the life insurance costs that the policy has charged during the time the policy has been in force. These costs therefore are paid on a pre-tax basis even when a policy is surrendered.

Four: Tax-Free Use of Untaxed Earnings and Gains

The fourth income tax benefit of life insurance depends on whether or not you incur taxation as a result of *using* the monies accumulated within the life insurance policy while it is still in force. You could use these monies by 1) withdrawing them, 2) borrowing them from the insurance company, or 3) pledging the policy as collateral for a loan. Prior to June 21, 1988, you could, if the policy permitted, withdraw from your life insurance policy an amount equal to what you had invested in the policy and not pay any income taxes on those funds. Uncle Sam considered the transaction a straight return of the policyowner's original investment and none of it was considered investment earnings. If you withdrew an amount exceeding the investment in the contract, the amount withdrawn above this basis was subject to ordinary income tax. As a result, you normally would withdraw from a policy no more than what you had put into it, and if you wanted to use additional funds that had accumulated in the policy you would make a loan against the policy or collateralize the policy in order to get at those funds without being taxed on them. Prior to June 21st, 1988, this could be done on almost any life insurance policy without paying income taxes on any of the accumulated gain within the contract.

The income tax benefits of life insurance are provided for

a purpose. They encourage people to buy life insurance policies which provide for family and business security. In 1986 Uncle Sam came down hard on all tax shelters. Life insurance appeared to be about the safest tax-advantaged investment that remained available. Insurance companies saw this too, and carefully designed their policies to maximize investment opportunity and minimize life insurance expenses in order to get the consumer's investment business. Insurance companies made policy loans attractive by charging a low rate of interest equal to the policyowner's earnings on funds inside of the policy that were collateralized by the loan. You could borrow money from an insurance company at 6% and they still would credit you with 6% on the amount borrowed. Thus you would have very little concern about the amount or duration of a policy loan. Policy loans are entirely a policyowner decision. This feature means that you can compound tax-deferred/tax-free and spend without current taxation—quite a deal!

Modified Endowment Insurance—TAMRA 88

Single premium life policies are the most investment-oriented life insurance policies. In effect they become maximum funded policies with the first—and only—premium. Prior to June 21, 1988, they combined 1) high returns, 2) a deferral or no tax on those returns, and 3) the ability to access those returns without current taxation. In 1988, Congress decided this was too much of a good thing. The result was that in November of 1988, the Technical and Miscellaneous Revenue Act of 1988 (TAMRA) was signed into law. This new law defined a new class of life insurance policies that Uncle Sam considered too investment-oriented, named modified endowment policies, and removed the tax-free accessibility to the cash in these policies. Any policy issued after June 20, 1988, that falls into the classification of a modified endowment policy cannot provide the policyowner with the privilege of withdrawing from, borrowing from, or collateralizing the values accrued within the policy without incurring immediate taxation on policy gains. Indeed, if the policyowner is under 59 1/2, not only do income taxes become due on the amount of gain accessed in the contract, but also a 10% penalty would be applicable to the amount included in gross income as a result of the withdrawal, borrowing or collateralization. The only exceptions to this penalty are if the funds are withdrawn as a result of disability or over a period a time related to the policy-owner's lifetime (annuitized).

How To Avoid "Modified Endowment" Status

We'll assume that you, the policyowner, want all four of the income tax benefits of life insurance, and in particular you want the ability to make withdrawals up to your basis or loans on your policy without being exposed to ordinary income tax or penalties. In order to accomplish this with a post-June 20th, 1988 policy, you may invest no more into your policy during the first seven policy years than an amount determined by the government-mandated test called the "seven-pay test." The seven-pay test has nothing to do with your having to pay seven premiums or your having to pay seven equal premiums. It concerns only the limitation on the amount that you can pay into your policy within the first seven years of its existence. For example, if the insurance company offering you a life insurance policy informs you (and, the insurance company *should* provide you with the information) that the seven-pay test allows no more than $1,000 per policy year, you could put up to, but no more than $1,000 into the policy in the first year. You could pay up to, but not more than, a total of $2,000 by the end of the second year. For the first seven policy years, the cumulative maximum you could contribute to the policy would be $7000. At that point your policy would have completed the testing period, would not be a modified endowment contract, and your accessibility to policy values by way of loans and withdrawals up to basis should not incur taxation or penalties. The amount of your contributions to your policy are also controlled by the other provisions of Internal Revenue Code Section 7702. Indeed, often you will find these other provisions are more restrictive in the fifth through seventh policy years than the seven-pay test restrictions, and you will not be able to contribute as much as the seven-pay test indicates. Your insurance company should inform you if your contributions exceed those allowed by the provisions of IRC Section 7702. You, however, will need to keep track of the seven-pay test limits of your policy and keep your investment below them based upon your policies anniversary dates.

Material Change to a Pre-June 21, 1988 Policy

The TAMRA '88 provisions also put restrictions on pre-June 21, 1988 policies if they are materially changed. The "material change" provision is likely to cause problems. Other than death benefit and future policy value increases resulting naturally from the payment of premiums that comply with the seven-pay test in the first seven contract years, and benefit increases resulting from investment and/or interest earnings on those premiums, *any change in a policy is likely to be deemed a material change.* A material change will result in the policy being considered a "new" contract entered into after June 20th, 1988, and subject to the seven-pay test as of the date the material change takes effect. The policy then must be tested under the 1988 rules. If it fails the test at any time in the following seven years, it will become a modified endowment contract (see the following section). Policies that can pass the seven-pay test are *not* modified endowments and retain *all* the tax benefits of life insurance. Be careful in making changes to your currently grandfathered pre-June 21, 1988 policies.

When to Ignore the Seven-Pay Test Limits

If you wish, you can still buy a single-premium policy, an investment-oriented policy, or a policy referred to by Uncle Sam as a "modified endowment" contract. Such policies still enjoy the tax-free death benefit of the total proceeds to be paid by the contract and the tax deferral on the inside buildup or earnings within the policy as a result of interest, dividends and/or capital gains. What's new for these policies is that now (post-June 20, 1988) if you borrow, withdraw or collateralize this policy, you will have to pay income taxes to the extent that you have gain in your policy and a 10% penalty on any amount of income included as a result of withdrawing, borrowing, or collateralizing your policy (the exceptions being disability or annuity pay-outs). If the inability to access the money within your policy without current taxation is *not* important to you, then the change in the law is irrelevant and you may continue to use these policies to accomplish your objectives. In the past, over 90% of the purchasers of single-premium policies have not borrowed from them. For those who do not use this money during life, the new rules will have no impact.

If you are not sure whether or not it will be necessary for you to access the money within your policy in the future, we recommend that you comply with the seven-pay test regulations. Make sure that your policy is not deemed a modified endowment contract so that you may keep the fourth advantage of life insurance available to you, tax and penalty free access to your cash.

Try the following. Using your own age, consult Figure 9–11. Look at the figures provided along side of your approximate age. A 40-year-old, for example, could invest $209 per $1,000 into a single premium life insurance policy and enjoy only the first three income tax benefits of the life insurance policy. $209 per $1,000 would mean a $20,900 investment into a $100,000 policy. That would be the only premium you would pay into that contract, and the funds would compound within that contract without current taxation for the rest of your life. At your death all of the death benefit, which may or may not include extra death benefits caused by the compound earnings within the policy, would be payable to your named beneficiary and there would be no income tax liability. However, should you borrow on, collateralize or withdraw from this policy, you would be taxed on the amount borrowed, withdrawn or collateralized to the extent of gain in the contract. You also would incur the 10% penalty if you are under 59 1/2 years of age. These same tax regulations would apply to any policy that you, as a 40-year-old

---

Figure 9–11
Life Insurance Premium Choices
(Annual premium per $1,000 face amount, male, non-smoker)

Age	Term Insur.	Target Univ. Life	Whole Life	Seven Pay	Maximum Single
30	.88	7.20	$ 11	$ 29	$135
40	1.13	11.40	15	42	209
50	3.16	18.70	22	60	314
60	6.63	31.50	36	83	446
70	25.92	51.10	70	114	592
75	55.39	64.20	102	135	665

Note: These are approximations and appropriate for illustration purposes only. For precise numbers for you and the policy you are considering, contact your insurance company.

---

policyowner, purchased that was above the seven-pay test maximum of $42 per $1,000, right up to the $210 per $1,000 maximum. If you paid only $43 per $1,000 into the policy, note that the seven-pay test maximum in Figure 9–11 is $42, the policy would be considered a modified endowment. However, if you limited yourself to paying no more than $42 per $1,000 per year into this policy for the first seven years, you would retain the ability to borrow on the policy without paying taxes or penalties on withdrawals, policy loans or col-lateralizations.

As you can see in Figure 9–12, Uncle Sam's 1988 regula-tions affected a very broad range of premium payments (for our 40-year-old, between $42 and $210 per $1,000 of face amount) and did an excellent job of eliminating the "abuse" that Uncle Sam was trying to eliminate: *the ability to earn tax-free and spend tax-free.* However, also note in Figure 9–13, that the normal 40-year-old buying a traditional whole life policy or a new universal life policy with what one would consider

Figure 9–12
Single Premium/7-Pay Maximum Premiums

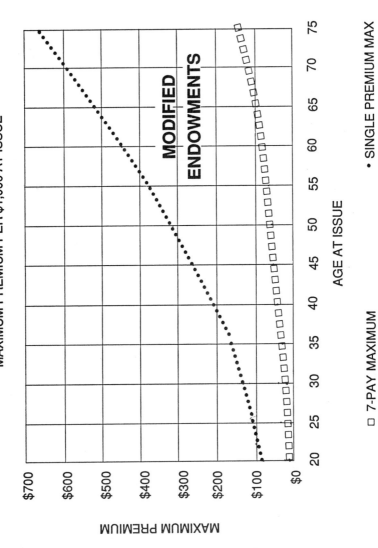

MAXIMUM PREMIUM PER $1,000 AT ISSUE

MODIFIED ENDOWMENTS

□ 7-PAY MAXIMUM   • SINGLE PREMIUM MAX

AGE AT ISSUE

MAXIMUM PREMIUM

an "adequate" funding level would, in most cases, only be paying $15 per $1,000 for a whole life policy, or $12 per $1,000 for a universal life policy. This means the 40-year-old can still invest almost three times what he would normally put into a term "plus" life insurance policy and retain all of the advantages of life insurance including accessibility to funds that have accumulated in the contract without current taxation. Before you buy, make sure that you know the limitations that apply to the policy you are considering.

Universal/Universal/Variable Death Benefit Options

When you apply for a universal or universal variable life policy, the application asks if you want your death benefit to be payable on Option A or Option B. (In some cases these may be labeled Option 1 or Option 2.) It is important that you select the proper option if you expect to maintain management control over the amount of life insurance your policy provides.

Option A

Option A is a death benefit option in which you stipulate to the insurance company the total amount of death benefit payable to your beneficiaries—for example, $200,000. If you stipulate Option A (or Option 1), your chosen level of premium payments and the investment results in your policy will have no impact on your death benefit. If you have elected $200,000 as your death benefit under an Option A, that's exactly what your beneficiaries will receive. If you had paid $50,000 worth of premiums and had investment results that doubled that amount, your account value would be $100,000. The insurance company would still pay off a total of $200,000, $100,000 of which would be your account value and $100,000 insurance company money. Option A minimizes life insurance costs, because every time your account value increases either with premium payments or positive investment results, the life insurance, or the amount at risk (the amount of insurance com-

Figure 9–13
7-Pay Maximum/Normal Premiums

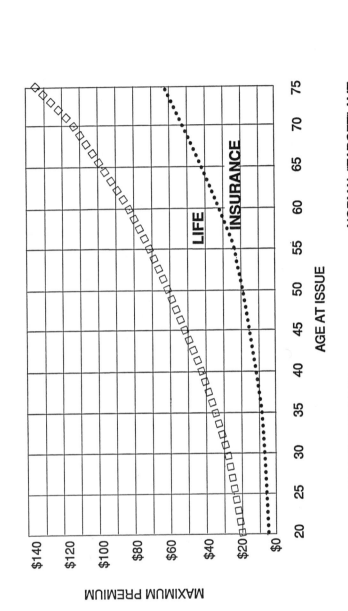

MAXIMUM PREMIUM PER $1,000 AT ISSUE

□ 7-PAY MAXIMUM   • NORMAL "TARGET" AMT

pany money that is to be paid to your beneficiaries in the event of your death), is reduced. When the amount at risk is reduced, your mortality charges are reduced.

With Option A, you lose control over the amount at risk. Also, good investment returns and capital you have accumulated in your policy become irrelevant when you die—good or bad, a lot or a little, $200,000 is the total payment. Let us say for example that you possess a $10,000 certificate of deposit and a $200,000 life insurance policy and you decide that the $10,000 would earn more inside of the policy than inside the certificate of deposit. You transfer $10,000 into the life insurance policy—but you die immediately thereafter. The insurance policy pays $200,000. The day before, while the CD was still in the bank, you had a $200,000 life insurance policy and a $10,000 CD and, had you died at that point, your beneficiary would have received both the $200,000 and the $10,000 CD. But, the instant the insurance company received your CD for deposit into an Option A policy, they reduced the amount of the death benefit they were providing by an amount equal to what they had received from you. Poor timing makes this a poor investment. For this reason, we recommend that during your accumulation years you avoid an Option A policy unless you have a specific reason for selecting this option.

Option B

When you elect Option B for your universal or universal/variable life insurance policy, you direct the insurance company to pay you the stipulated benefit from *its* money, not yours. Instead of having the $200,000 death benefit include the investment account, you ask that your investment account be paid in addition to the amount at risk of $200,000. By electing Option B in the example above, when the individual transferred the $10,000 into his investment account, that investment account would increase by $10,000. In the event of death, the life insurance, $200,000, (the amount at risk) *and* the investment account ($10,000) would be paid to the beneficiary for a total of $210,000.

One might criticize this strategy by saying that mortality charges under Option B will be higher than under Option A. This is certainly true because the more insurance company money you demand, the higher the mortality costs will be. However, you maintain control. If you want the insurance company to reduce the amount at risk, all you have to do is to direct the insurance company to reduce the face amount of your policy to your predetermined level. They will do so and thereby reduce your mortality costs.

Be cautious in asking for any reductions in the death benefit of your life insurance policy, particularly during the first 15 years of the policy's life. Uncle Sam has stipulated the maximum amount of premium or investment that you may have in a particular life insurance policy and that amount is related to the death benefit under the contract. If you have a substantial investment and you direct the insurance company to reduce your death benefit, you may find that they can do so only if they give you back some of the cash within your policy. This is referred to as "force out." Force out means there is too much cash in relation to the face amount of your policy. The insurance company is forced to take money out of the policy and return it to you to remain in compliance with the definition of life insurance in IRC 7702. Money forced out in this manner will trigger ordinary income tax on the amount forced out to the extent of gain in the policy. Our recommendation is to utilize Option B in your contracts, avoid a reduction of face amount during the first 15 years of your policy life (do so only *after* ascertaining that it will not create tax problems), and thereafter do so only with a great deal of caution. Consider the potential income tax implication of your changes. Work closely with your insurance company and other advisors in order to avoid income tax surprises.

Using the Money in Your Policy—Withdrawals or Policy Loans

The rule of thumb when you need cash from your policy is to use a policy loan in lieu of a withdrawal. This recommendation is based upon the assumption that the universal or universal/variable policy you own is working for you and that you are satisfied with the investment results within the policy. However, you may have a temporary need for cash. A temporary need for cash infers that you probably will replace those funds into the policy at some future date. The question is, will those funds be subject to the state premium tax when they are put back into the policy? Funds will be subject to the state premium tax if they are considered premium. If you withdraw from your policy and later put the money back into the policy, that is considered premium and subject to state premium tax. Whereas, if you borrow from your policy and pay off your policy loan, that is not premium, and is not subject to state premium tax. As a result, a policy loan usually is preferable to a policy withdrawal in order to avoid the reimposition of state premium taxes. If, however, you intend to take the funds from the insurance policy and keep them out for a substantial period of time, you will have to pay interest on the loan offset by the interest the insurance company credits on the amount collateralized in your policy. You probably will pay the insurance company one or two percent more than they pay you. This cost could amount to more than the reimposition of state premium taxes and make a withdrawal less expensive than a loan. In order to determine which would be most advantageous to you, balance the net cost of the policy loan against the state premium tax that would be incurred if you were to withdraw and pay back that withdrawal at a future date.

Investing in Life Insurance

If you choose what I consider to be the most manageable of the manageable life insurance policies—the universal/variable contract—I would recommend that you determine the amount at risk that you require and purchase a universal variable life insurance policy using Option B adequately funding your contract. Strive to optimally fund your contract utilizing a guaranteed principal, guaranteed interest account so that your investment would generate interest earnings sufficient to pay all of your mortality and expense charges. Once this optimum funding level has been reached you can utilize the other mutual funds and/or the guaranteed principal, guaranteed interest account to help you accomplish your other financial objectives.

Near-Term, Specific Purpose Money

The guaranteed interest, guaranteed principal account can be used as an emergency fund or a place to accumulate funds for some important purpose that will occur within a year or two. The funds can be available to you by means of a policy loan in most cases within ten days of your request. In the typical universal/variable policies you will find a variety of funds that will accomplish this important, near-term investment objective. Other than a guaranteed principal, guaranteed interest account you could use the money market fund or even the high-yield fund with short maturity date securities. Match the fund objectives to your objectives. The capital you invest should earn competitive interest rates without current taxation and still be available for your use for any number of near-term purposes such as college educations, the down payment on a home or the purchase of an automobile. In these days of non-deductible consumer loans, it makes good sense to pre-fund auto payments. Make car payments in advance into your policy where they compound without current taxation and then borrow from the policy when you want to buy the car. You can pay this loan off by continuing to make car payments into this account. Cash will then compound without taxation and be available in the account when your car needs to be replaced. This strategy eliminates automobile loans which generate non-deductible interest. It turns the situation around, generating compound interest that is not taxable to you. To use your policy like this you will want to invest no more than the amount allowed by the seven-pay test (see Figure 9–11).

College Education, Retirement and/or Net Worth Build-up

Where and how do you accumulate funds for those college

Figure 9–14

	Period 1	Period 2	Period 3	Period 4	Period 5	Totals
Amount Invested	$100	$100	$100	$100	$100	= $500
Share Market Value at Purchase	$100	$50	$25	$50	$100	
Number of Shares Purchased	1	2	4	2	1	= 10 Shares

Market Value of Fund
In Period 5

10 Shares X $100 Market Value
= $1,000
Minus Cost $500
Gain $500

educations that will arrive in seven, ten, or fifteen years? What about retirement? How can you increase your net worth so that you and your family are more secure? One way is to use dollar cost averaging. With dollar cost averaging you invest a set amount into an investment at specified intervals of time. Figure 9–14 presents a five-period dollar cost averaging strategy using $100 per period with dramatic decreases and increases in unit value during the accumulation period.

Dollar cost averaging enables you to invest in volatile investments, such as common stocks, and to avoid failed investments. This strategy is not likely to generate instant investment returns—but you are likely to grow rich *slowly* if you practice it consistently over long periods.

The various mutual funds offered by your universal/variable policies are perfectly suited for dollar cost averaging strategies. Your insurance company will bill you monthly so that you may direct regular payments among the various mutual funds. No income taxes are charged against your accumulated funds. You may make the payments to a common fund, rather than earmarking funds separately for each child. People who allocate investments to individual children often find themselves with one child who has a large education fund and no desire to continue schooling, and another child who has a small education fund but a great desire to attend college. It can, and does, create problems. The strategy of accumulating unallocated education funds makes it much easier for a family to use the money where and when it is needed and, if it is not needed, to retain it for retirement security—all without current income taxation.

How to Disinvest in Life Insurance—When to Sell

If you do adopt a strategy of dollar cost averaging, your investment results will start out slowly and unimpressively. In fact, the more unimpressive the better because it may mean that the fund you have chosen is currently not popular or stocks are out of favor and therefore you are accumulating units at a low price. One thing is certain about the securities market: it goes up and it goes down. That which is out of favor comes back in favor, and that which is in favor goes out of favor. If you allow time—and this is a big and important *if*—well managed funds will one day come into favor. With consistent investing, you will accumulate a block of investment capital that *you* will define one day as significant. At that time you may decide that you do not wish to risk losing what you have accumulated. If so, sell off the volatile mutual fund in your policy at one of the "in favor" times and move the funds to a less volatile or lower risk account within the policy, but continue dollar cost averaging into the more volatile accounts. I suggest that when your gains are significant to you, *take them!* This strategy could be referred to as "Nibble and Nab"—nibble at the stock market via dollar cost averaging and nab your earnings when you consider them significant for your purposes.

Is this the fastest and best way to invest and accumulate? Not the fastest—it can be compared to flying an airplane; hours of boredom interspersed with moments of euphoria and terror . . . but statistically speaking it will get you there. The best? it is, if it enables you to do what you otherwise would not have been able to do.

It will be necessary for you to accumulate capital for your own retirement in order to supplement whatever income may be provided to you through your employer-provided plan, social security or other governments programs for which you qualify. Retirement is a long-term accumulation objective which, over the accumulation period, will be exposed to many risks. Inflation is one of the most substantial risks affecting the sufficiency of your retirement accumulations. Inflation constantly erodes the adequacy of your income. Prices rise over time, and if your income stays at a fixed level, you will find yourself a very unhappy retiree. You have to deal with this risk directly with your investment and accumulation strategy. This strategy will inevitably include the ownership of a diverse portfolio of common stocks. Your universal/variable life insurance policy gives you the opportunity to accumulate, own, and buy and sell stock mutual funds among the family of funds offered within your insurance policy, and to do it all without having your returns diminished by current income taxes.

There are now insurance contract tracking services such as "Insurance Investing" by the Douglas Fabian Company of Huntington Beach, California, that guide investors to stock funds during market rises and out of them during market dips. There are also asset allocation accounts offered by life insurance companies that will help you allocate funds among the mutual funds available depending upon your objectives and willingness to accept risk.

In short, a quality universal/variable life policy that can do all that we have described should eventually be a core holding in most family situations. It should be used to the maximum extent the economic circumstances of the family allow.

In order to monitor your strategy, we recommend that each year you fill in the blanks in Figure 9–15, your Funding Finder Worksheet.

When considering a new universal or universal/variable policy for purchase make sure that the numbers for the four top boxes are based upon reasonable assumptions that have been explained to you and that you understand and accept.

Once you have purchased one of these policies, you will receive an annual report that contains the actual results for the past policy year. Extract the four numbers for the top blanks from that annual report.

Fill in numbers for expenses, mortality costs, investment results and premium paid, then fill in expenses and the mortality costs in the spaces provided in the left column. Next, determine if your premium and/or investment results for the year are less than, equal to, or exceed the amount of expenses and mortality costs. Once you have determined their relationship to policy cost, fill in the appropriate column with the appropriate numbers. This will show you the funding strategy you have been using for the past year. Then, take control! Decide what funding strategy you will adopt for the coming year based upon your needs, resources and objectives.

Figure 9–15
Baldwin Funding Finder Worksheet

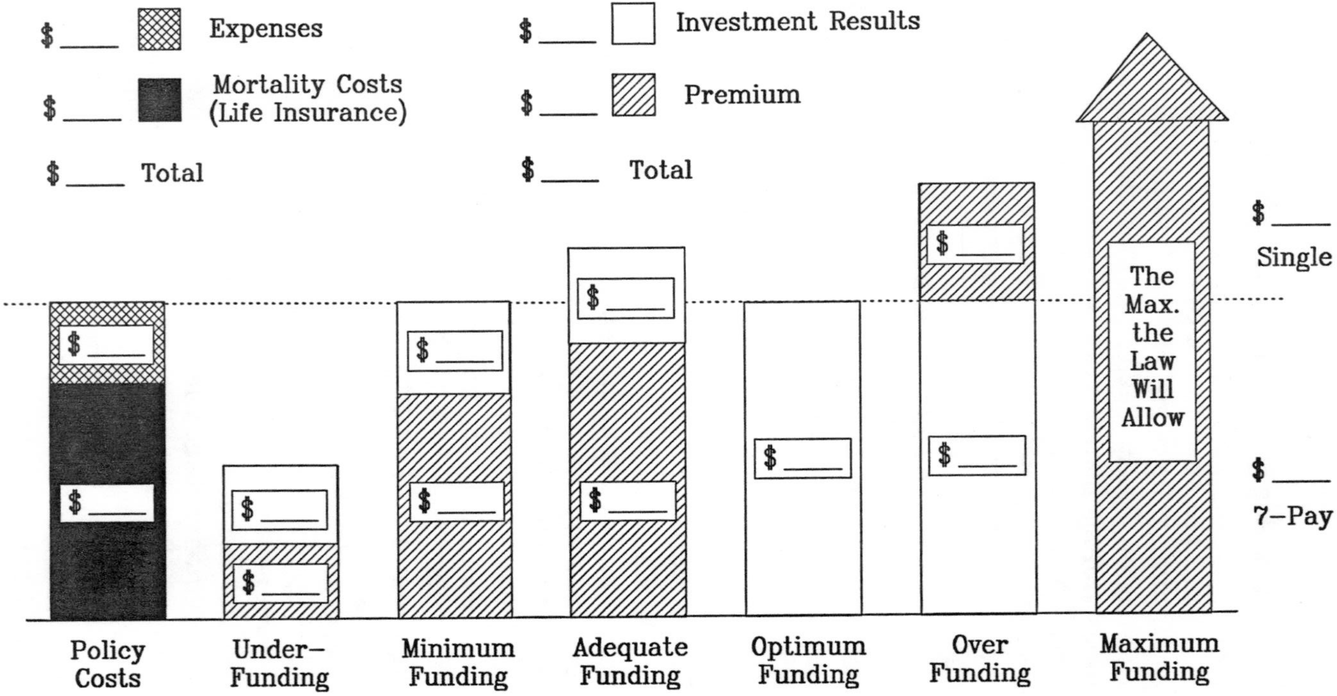

Legend:
- ▨ Expenses
- ▨ Mortality Costs (Life Insurance)
- $ ___ Total
- □ Investment Results
- ▨ Premium
- $ ___
- $ ___
- $ ___ Total

Columns:
- Policy Costs
- Under-Funding
- Minimum Funding
- Adequate Funding
- Optimum Funding
- Over Funding
- Maximum Funding

The Max. the Law Will Allow

Single

7-Pay

TEN

ANNUITIES

We have discussed the three basic elements of a life insurance policy: the expenses, mortality charges and, when selected, the investment account. The investment account is unique in that it can grow without current taxation. The investment account of the annuity contract also is allowed to grow within the contract without current taxation and it also includes a charge for expenses. It is, however, without significant mortality charges. Many variable annuities do include a mortality charge of approximately six-tenths of one percent, which provides that in the event of the annuitant's death the beneficiary of the annuity will receive the greater of the investment in the contract or the annuity's account value. This provides death protection in case of poor investment results. Other than this minor safety net for beneficiaries, annuity contracts are oriented to benefit the purchaser rather than beneficiaries. Life insurance, on the other hand, is oriented for the benefit of the beneficiary. The beneficiary of the life insurance contract is "other than the insured." Let's relate that to an annuity contract.

The annuity contract could be defined as a life insurance

211

policy without the mortality charges because there is no "net amount at risk." The basic elements of the contract are two: 1) the tax deferred investment account and 2) the expenses associated with the contract. The primary objective of the annuity contract is to pay investment returns to the annuitant, not to pay tax-free death benefits to others. You would use it either to accumulate money to be used at some future date, usually in retirement, or to provide for the systematic payment of monies that you have accumulated. The three primary distinctions between the annuity contract and the life insurance contract are: 1) the annuity contract has no significant mortality charges, 2) annuities have no "net amount at risk," and 3) the annuity contract is *not* paid tax-free to a beneficiary at the annuitant's death.

The annuity contract loses all of its tax-deferral if it has not been used up prior to the annuitant's death. It can be passed to a beneficiary, but any income tax liabilities in the contract go with it and become income tax liabilities for the beneficiary of the contract. Spouses of annuitants may be able to continue the contract and continue to enjoy tax deferred earnings but non-spouse beneficiaries are forced to begin distribution and thus pay taxes.

Note in Figure 10–1 that we have diagramed annuities and labeled the right side of the diagram Accumulation Annuities and the left side Payout Annuities.

People usually think of annuities only as "payout" annuities because of their ability to pay out a systematic monthly income as retirement income to an annuitant. In fact, the term *annuity*, is defined in the dictionary as "an amount payable yearly or at other regular intervals for a certain or uncertain period." It defines the annuitant as one who receives benefits or payments from an annuity or who is entitled to receive such benefits. Employers frequently pay pension and retirement benefits as an annuity. They offer the retiree varying monthly incomes depending upon the guarantees made as to what will happen to the payment should the annuitant die. Since this is the most common use of annuities, it is easy to understand why most people think of them in these terms.

Figure 10-1

ANNUITIES

A PAYOUT VEHICLE

AN ACCUMULATION VEHICLE

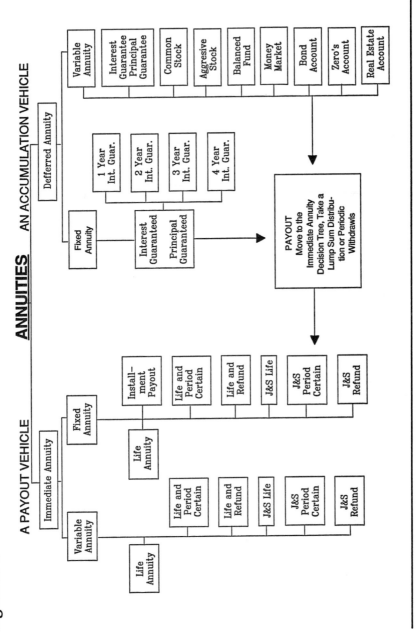

The other side of annuities, however, is their ability to act as vehicles to accumulate capital for future use without current income taxation on interest, dividends or capital gains within the annuity contract. More and more people now use annuities as a way to accumulate capital to supplement their pension and social security incomes in the future.

An annuity contract is not a particular investment in and of itself. The annuity contract is, so to speak, a wrapper around investments. You may wrap an annuity contract around many types of investments varying from very conservative investments, such as guaranteed-principal, guaranteed-interest accounts, to relatively aggressive investments such as aggressive stock accounts, high-yield bond accounts, or anywhere in between. Annuities may contain families of mutual funds that will determine whether the annuity contract is very conservative or very aggressive. Annuity contracts are not inherently either risky or safe, aggressive or conservative. They may be controlled. The primary function of annuities is assisting you to either accumulate or spend your retirement capital. These contracts can be adapted to almost everyone's needs.

Payout/Immediate Annuities

Fixed Period or Fixed Amount

As you look at the decision tree under "Immediate Annuity" in Figure 10–1, you will find that the first decision you must make when purchasing an annuity is whether it is to be fixed or variable. The payment of the fixed annuity, the periodic check issued to the annuitant, will be in a fixed amount for the duration of the payout period. The duration of the payout period may be determined by stipulating to the insurance company the period of time during which you wish to receive the checks. For example, you may request that checks be sent monthly for the next 10 years. At the end of that time, the payments would terminate. Based upon the amount of money available, prevailing levels of interest rates and the period of time you select, the insurance company will determine the amount of your periodic check. Alternatively, you could request checks of $1,000 per month for as long as you have funds available from the accumulated value in your annuity contract. In this case, the company would determine how many months they would be able to pay the $1,000 per month, based upon the same factors.

For Life

You might be concerned that your money will run out before you do—that your capital will be exhausted before you die. If so, you would ask the insurance company to have the monthly checks continue for life. This seems very reassuring—but what if you die after just one check has been paid? The checks do indeed terminate at death, and any capital remaining in the annuity contract would be forfeited to the insurance company. In this case you, the annuitant, take that risk. You usually will receive a greater income than someone who demanded more in the way of guarantees from the insurance company than those promised by a life annuity. Alternatively, you could order the insurance company to make payments for life, but to continue those payments for some stipulated period of time if you should die early. For example, you could insist the insurance company make payments for life with a minimum period of at least 10, 15 or 20 years, or until you or your beneficiary had received back at least the entire amount that you had originally invested in the contract with the insurance company. The latter is referred to as a refund annuity.

Insurance companies can guarantee payments for the lives of two people. These are referred to as *joint and survivor annuities* and are used most frequently by married couples. Joint and survivor annuities can also be issued with minimum guarantee periods such as the 10-, 15- or 20-years certain variety, or the refund-certain variety.

Should You "Annuitize"?

Annuitizing may be defined as contracting for a series of payments from an annuity. There are three risks involved. The first we have just discussed—the risk that you die too early and/or select the wrong guarantee and do not receive back from the insurance company what you could have, had you not accepted the monthly payout arrangement. The second risk is that once you have informed the insurance company which payout you will accept, there is no turning back once they have issued the contract and you have cashed the first check. From that point on, your checks will keep coming in exactly as you originally requested. If that proves to be inappropriate or indeed disastrous, to you personally as a result of some change in your economic status, the annuity contract still cannot be changed. The third risk is that the amount of the check in a fixed annuity will be the same each month for the duration of the annuity period. If prices increase at five percent per year, the dollars that you receive from your annuity will purchase five percent less each year that you receive income from the contract. This decrease in your purchasing power will mean a reduction in your standard of living each year that you live. You may receive a check that purchases a $1,000 worth of goods in 1989, but 21 years later in the year 2010 that same check will purchase a 1989 equivalent of only $340.56 worth of goods assuming 5% inflation. Your standard of living would have been cut to one-third of what it was when you retired. This is a major risk for retirees.

Many employer-provided retirement plans will not give you the choice of whether or not to annuitize, but merely the opportunity to choose among the various types of annuity guarantees. You would have to determine the income generated by the various alternatives, adapt those alternatives to your personal situation and select the one best suited to your family's needs. It is easier to advise which annuities *not* to select than it is which ones to select so do your decision making backwards—cross out the selections you do not like. For, example, if you are in very poor health, you would not elect a life annuity without a guarantee period. In fact, you probably would choose the longest guarantee period to provide the greatest payout available. If you were sick but your spouse was healthy, a joint and 100% survivor annuity may be an obvious choice. Each situation is different. Your choice must be based upon the facts and circumstances as they stand on the day your decision must be made.

Annuitize or Take a Lump Sum?

How do you decide whether to annuitize or to take a lump sum cash disbursement? The first step is to determine the amount of the payout, what the lump sum cash disbursement could best be used for and how much would be left to invest, net after taxes. If you don't have a particular opportunity to exploit with this money, then consider rolling it into an individual IRA account. That would conserve the principal from which you could draw interest earnings but you would not have to annuitize. You could then compare the income that would be generated from the earnings in the IRA funds to the income offered under the payout annuity arrangements offered by your employer. The younger you are when you retire, the more likely you are to find that the interest earnings on an IRA account are almost equivalent to the monthly income offered by the employer on an annuitized basis. The amount of income generated on the annuitized basis should exceed what you are able to receive in an arrangement where you use only the interest on your capital sum, not the principal. The annuity, after all, is making payments to you of both principal and interest. If there is little difference in income, the fact that the rollover IRA, not annuitized, conserves your principal and your flexibility for the future makes it an attractive alternative. You are not locked in to any particular monthly payment, you may get at your principal, and you may change your mind in the future.

Why would you annuitize? You might be forced to do so if it was the only way to provide sufficient income for your family's survival. It may not be possible for you to conserve principal in a rollover IRA. It would be preferable for everyone would have sufficient pension income, social security income and personal assets to prevent them from having to annuitize. Annuitization puts your income at risk of being eroded by inflation, having the principal forfeited to an insurance company because of premature death and it eliminates the possibility of changing the contract to suit your needs that change in the future. However, funds may not always be sufficient to maintain this "best of all possible worlds."

Suppose you do use the IRA rollover strategy and try to survive by withdrawing just the interest from your IRA account. You may find that after a year or two the interest earnings are not providing enough income. As a result of being older, it is highly likely that the income when you annuitize will be higher than it would have been when you originally retired. Annuities are based on your life expectancy and, therefore, as you get older, the insurance company is able to pay you more. When dealing with immediate annuities the consequences of waiting, as long as you are careful to conserve principal, are not detrimental. It pays to compare when purchasing a lifetime income. Ask a number of the highest quality insurance companies what they will pay you based upon the immediate annuity and the guarantees that you require in that immediate annuity. There can be substantial differences in what various companies will offer, and you might even be able to do better than what your employer is offering you. Your immediate Annuity Action Letter will help you to get the information you need to make a decision (see Figure 10–2).

The decision to annuitize a capital sum can be a very emotional one. Seek the counsel of a trusted and objective financial advisor, your CPA, attorney, the trust officer at the bank, and especially the professional insurance company salesperson who can help you come up with the numbers. These people can examine your situation and suggest alternatives that you may not have considered.

Immediate Variable Annuities

The decision tree in Figure 10–1 also has a "variable annuity" branch. The variable annuity was intended to overcome the objection to the decrease in purchasing power that is the inherent risk in a fixed annuity as a result of inflation. Anyone dependent on a fixed annuity income for a lifetime can look forward to an ever-decreasing standard of living in an inflationary economy. The idea behind a variable annuity is to invest the capital sum of the annuity into a portfolio of common stocks anticipating that inflation will cause the common stocks to appreciate and that appreciation will allow for increasing income to the annuitant. Annuitants have not found these variable annuities very attractive. First, there is risk inherent in the variable annuity. You do not know which way the stock market will go. You cannot be sure that the annuity will produce increased income as inflation increases. During the hyper-inflation of 1979 and 1980, the stock market performed very poorly, and variable annuities did not offset the effect of inflation with commensurate increases in income. Secondly, variable annuities do not satisfy the demand for maximum consistent monthly income that most people who annuitize are seeking. For example, the author put a variable annuity in force with a portion of a relative's retirement capital. The contract was established in 1972 to pay $100 per month based upon the performance of the underlying stock account. Payments were disappointing during the first ten years of the policy's existence—getting as low as $72 per month. The annuitant was not thrilled with what we had done; however, by the time she died in 1986, payments had risen as high as $262 per month. Unfortunately, by that time she could not enjoy the increase as much as she could have in her younger years. For these reasons, not very many variable immediate annuities are sold.

Accumulation/Deferred Annuities

Do you like the investment results of some of the investments you have right now? Would you like those investment results even more if you did not have to pay income tax on them currently but could defer taxes until some future date? If the answer to both questions is yes, it is highly likely that there is a deferred annuity that will mirror the investment results that you are obtaining in that taxable investment.

When people first think of deferred annuities as an accumulation vehicle, they usually think of fixed interest. Most people who buy this type of product use the guaranteed principal and guaranteed interest accounts. A fixed income alternative is available in some variable annuities. A variable annuity contract is not necessarily more risky than a fixed annuity contract. The degree of risk that you take as an annuitant is dependent upon the account or accounts that you choose to use. Utilizing the fixed annuity limits you to fixed interest investments only, so your investment decisions will be based upon how long an interest rate guarantee you would like to have. If you knew which way interest rates would go in the future, you not only would be very wealthy, but you also could choose which interest rate guarantee period would be most beneficial to you. If interest rates are at their peak and are inevitably going to go down, then you would like to lock in the high interest rates for the longest period available. Alternatively, if interest rates are at a low point and are inevitably going to go up, you would seek to have a short guarantee period so that as soon as it expired, you could renew the contract at a higher interest rate. However, you cannot know the future levels of interest rates, and errors can be costly. An incorrect decision can leave you with little flexibility and returns that do not offset inflation. Fixed annuities are a single-dimension, interest rate-sensitive investment. As such, they are appropriate for a limited amount of your portfolio, but not your *total* portfolio. A lack of diversification in this area can cause significant decreases in your purchasing power as a result of inflation.

Your alternative is a variable annuity. As shown in Figure 10–1, there are a number of investment accounts available in variable annuities today. The advantage of the variable annuity is that you can utilize the various accounts available in the contract for personal purposes. You can move assets from the stock account to the guaranteed interest account when the stock market is up, thereby locking in your capital gains, and you can do it without having to be bothered with income tax considerations. There is no question about it—we can build wealth faster if we don't have to share it with Uncle Sam.

The other side of this coin is that losses inside of annuity contracts cannot be deducted currently, which makes them inappropriate investment vehicles for those long-term investments that have a higher probability of resulting in losses. Your high-risk investments belong outside of annuity contracts when the major benefit of such investments may be the deductibility of the losses.

Non-Qualified IRAs

Use a deferred annuity instead of a non-qualified IRA. Mind you, a tax deductible contribution to an IRA account—which can easily be included inside of a tax-deferred annuity—is something that we *always* recommend. However, a non-qualified IRA is something we always recommend that people avoid. If you can't deduct your IRA contribution, don't make one. The only advantage of a non-qualified IRA is the tax deferral available as a result of it being an IRA contract. As you can see, that same tax deferral is available in a regular annuity contract or a life insurance policy. The advantages of the regular annuity contract as opposed to the IRA are that there are no government restrictions on the amount that you can put in the contract, you need not file a IRS Form 536 with your tax return, nor must you follow the incredible instructions provided in IRS Publication 509 on how to pay taxes on your non-qualified IRA when combined with your qualified IRA. Additionally, the non-qualified annuity does not have substantial IRS penalties for errors, as do non-qualified IRA accounts. There are no redeeming features in a non-qualified IRA that can make-up for the IRS hassle factor involved in those investments.

Pre-59 1/2 Withdrawals

The deferred annuity, used as an accumulation vehicle, is protected from current income taxation because Uncle Sam assumes these accumulations are for your retirement security. He is not interested in providing you with tax benefits for money that you take from your annuity contract prior to the age 59 1/2. In fact, if you make withdrawals prior to that age not only will you have to pay taxes on the amount withdrawn to the extent of earnings in the contract, but you will also have to pay a 10% penalty on amounts included in your gross income. After age 59 1/2, withdrawals are subject to income tax, but not the 10% penalty. The pre-age 59 1/2 exceptions to the penalty are distributions as a result of your death, disability or distributions taken under one of the life income options.

To Annuitize or Not To Annuitize

I suggest that you make sure that your annuity contract does not force you into annuitization until as late as possible, preferably age 85. Use your annuity contract in retirement like you would use a checkbook. Take funds from the contract when you need them, accepting the tax liability. Don't take funds in those years when you don't need the income, thus deferring the income tax liability. An annuity contract that can be managed in this fashion gives you a great deal of flexibility for planning withdrawals consistent with your needs and income tax planning.

Not annuitizing allows you to retain the advantage of controlling your income tax liability through continued deferral and periodic withdrawals from your annuity contract. It also gives you continued flexibility over the investment of the capital held within your annuity contract and you do not risk forfeiture of any capital to the insurance company in the event of death, as you do under "payout" annuity arrangements.

The disadvantages of the continual deferral and periodic withdrawal strategy is that the income available to you may not be as great (if you are not diminishing principal) as it would be if you annuitized. In addition, under the withdrawal method all that you take out of your post-August 14th, 1982 annuity will be taxable income until you have withdrawn all interest in the contract. Pre-August 14th, 1982 annuity investments can usually be withdrawn principal first (no tax) and interest last (taxable).

Under the annuitization method, each payment that you take is part principal and part interest. Frequently the tax-free return of principal of your annuitized monthly income will be between 40 and 50% of the total check that you receive. The annuitization method, therefore, is not only likely to generate more income than the interest-only method, but almost half of that income is likely to be exempt from income tax. It can give you greater after-tax income to spend.

Immediate Annuity Action Letter

Now that you have a basic understanding of accumulation and immediate annuity contracts, it's time to go shopping. The appropriate annuity depends upon your objectives and those of your spouse if you are married, in addition to your health situation and the capital available. With all of this in mind, you need to know the actual dollar amounts that the annuity could provide to you in your situation. This information is easy to obtain by adapting the action letter (Figure 10–2) to your personal situation and sending it to the insurance companies from whom you would consider purchasing an annuity contract. Based upon the information you provide, they will be happy to give you a quote to provide you, free of charge, information regarding what their contracts will do for you. Don't hesitate to ask all of your questions; you need to understand what you are considering buying.

The information you gather as a result of sending the action letter will assist you in making a decision regarding your employer provided retirement plan options. It also will give you the information you need in order to purchase an immediate annuity. Discuss the plans that seem to meet your family objectives with your financial advisors and a quality insurance professional. Since interest rates change frequently, the quotes that you receive will only be valid for a short period of time. Last months quote—or even last week's—may no longer be good today.

An immediate annuity contract is relatively simple because it is so inflexible. It promises you only the amount of the check that you are going to receive, how often you are

Figure 10–2
Immediate Annuity Action Letter

Gentlemen:

I am considering the purchase of an immediate annuity contract. I am interested in purchasing a single premium immediate *fixed/variable* annuity contract. The annuitant is a male/female born _____. I also would like a quote on a male/female born _____.

In addition to the above quotes, I would like a quote on a joint life annuity for a male/female born _____ and a male/female born _____. We are residents of the state of _____ and our personal marginal state and federal income tax bracket is _____%. Please base your quotes on a single consideration of $_____ and/or a monthly income of $_____ per month. The monies that I would be investing in this immediate annuity contract are coming from my personal funds/IRA funds/TSA funds/lump sum distribution from my employers qualified retirement plan or _____.

For quote purposes, please assume the insurance company would receive these proceeds by _____ (date). I would ask that my monthly payments begin _____ (date). (This date should be at least one month after the date that the insurance company receives the proceeds).

Please provide me with quotes from _____ [number of] insurance companies and send a Best's rating report on each insurance company that is providing a quote.

Mail the information to me at the following address. I will call you with my questions after I have had a chance to review the information. If you have any questions, please call me at _____.

Thank you very much for your assistance.

Sincerely,

Name
Address
Phone Number

going to receive it, and for how long. Therefore, you will be looking for the maximum amount of income based on the on the guarantees that you require of the insurance company.

The financial strength of the insurance company from whom you buy your annuity is very important. If you are going to succeed financially the insurance company must also. Demand quality. Deal with well-known, large household names in the insurance industry that have been keeping their promises to policyowners over a significant number of years. (The quality of insurance companies is discussed further in Chapter Eleven.) One way for you to obtain information in regard to a particular company is from a Best's report. You will note that a summary of the most current Best's report is requested in the action letter. Those reports will tell you the company's size and history, and will rate that company with a letter grade. We suggest that you purchase an annuity contract only from an insurance company rated A or A+ by Best. Although the Best's ratings are not infallible, they are a good starting point.

Deferred Annuity Action Letter

A deferred/accumulation annuity on the other hand, is a more complex purchase since the contract can be far more flexible. Generally speaking, if you are going to invest in a deferred annuity, you should seek flexibility. The most successful deferred annuity contracts are typically those that stay in existence over a long period of time. Your needs and attitudes inevitably will change over time, so you will want a contract that is adaptable to such change. If the annuity contract is inflexible, it is likely that you would either terminate it, trade it for another annuity contract, or put in a drawer. Any one of these three options might result in fees, penalties, potential tax liability and the losses that occur due to inattention. It is preferable to avoid such costs. The action letter in Figure 10–3 will indicate to the insurance company your specifications for a deferred annuity quote based upon your personal situation and requirements for a deferred annuity contract.

Figure 10–3
Deferred/Accumulation Annuity "Requests"

Gentlemen:

I am considering investing in a deferred annuity. I would prefer an annuity contract that allows me the flexibility of investing at my personal convenience when funds became available for investment. I would prefer not to purchase a contract that makes investment in the contract mandatory over some pre-determined time. I prefer not to accept the restrictions imposed by a single-premium deferred annuity contract unless such a contract would offer superior returns or features different than those available from a flexible premium annuity contract. For quote purposes, please use $_____ as my initial investment into the contract.

Please provide an explanation of any and all charges that will be made against my investment and the net amount that will go to work for me in the annuity contract. Also, please indicate any surrender charges or contingent withdrawal fees that I could be exposed to should I cash in the annuity contract and the period in which these charges are applicable.

I am not unfavorably disposed toward variable annuity contracts as long as there is a safe haven account available within the contract. Please indicate which account is a safe haven account and what guarantees of principal and interest are available within that account. I would also like to know if there are any restrictions on my movement into and/or out of any accounts during the life of the annuity contract. Please provide me with the prospectus and all other information that is available regarding all of the accounts within the contract.

I would like an annuity contract from a quality company with low expense and sales charges. I would prefer surrender charges to front- end sales charges so that all of my money would go to work for me immediately and so that, if I maintain my contract until after the surrender charge period, I may never have to pay such sales charges. I would like maximum flexibility, a good safe-haven account providing interest and principal guarantees, and good-performing, alternative mutual fund types of accounts. I seek flexibility and convenience of investment and frequent and convenient reporting regarding account balances. I would like to be able to switch between the various accounts at my convenience, preferably by telephone.

At this time, it is my intention to defer the annuity for as long a period as possible so please let me know at what age the insurance company insists that I begin to take funds. I would like to avoid forced annuitization for as long as possible. Please state explicitly any penalties I could be exposed to if I choose never to annuitize my contract. Please send the information to me at the address indicated below. Call me if there is anything else you need to know in order to provide me with this information.

Thank you for your assistance.

Sincerely,

Name
Address
Phone

This action letter specifically does not ask for an illustration regarding how your money might compound based on some particular investment or interest rate. The return from your annuity investment will be based upon maximizing interest rates and investment returns over a long period of time, as well as minimization of expenses. Your product evaluation should be directed toward the specific information regarding all expenses and charges that may be incurred under a particular contract as well as the investment and interest rate track record.

Once you establish a contract with acceptable expenses and charges and an acceptable portfolio of investment accounts (including an account that will provide a safe haven for guaranteeing principal and interest), what you do with it will determine its long-term performance. Basically you are seeking flexibility, good reporting and ease of management. Figure 10–4 is a list of questions that you will want to ask regarding your deferred annuity contract prior to purchase.

Use deferred annuity contracts in situations where you want deferral of taxation on investment earnings and the safety and security offered by the quality insurance company backing your contract. Consider a deferred annuity contract for the investment of personal funds in lieu of an investment in a non-qualified IRA. Since the appeal of a non-qualified IRA is the deferral of taxation which is also available within the deferred annuity contract, should you limit yourself to the non-qualified IRA rules? With the non-qualified IRA, you are limited to a maximum of $2,000 per year, current reporting, confusing tax calculations at eventual payout, forced payouts, and penalties if you happen to err. Alternatively, the non-qualified annuity contract gives you the same tax deferral, has no maximum limit, does not require current reporting, has straightforward tax calculations at eventual payout, a longer deferral period potential and no penalties. Deferred annuities are *good* investment vehicles for your long-term retirement capital accumulation—your core retirement assets as you get older.

Make sure that your qualified annuity contracts (those from your IRAs, retirement plan rollovers, and such) are ar-

Figure 10–4
Annuity Purchase Checklist

1. The company issuing the contract. The financial strength and track record of the insurance company is of paramount importance in today's financial world. An annuity contract is only successful when the relationship is long-term, i.e., lifetime.

2. Current interest rate, if you choose a fixed dollar annuity. Investment account, investment management and competitive interest and guaranteed principal accounts if you choose a variable annuity.

3. Guarantee period for the guaranteed interest rate.

4. Minimum guaranteed rate of interest after the initial guarantee period is complete.

5. Bail-out provisions. Provisions that allow you to surrender the annuity contract without penalty if the interest rate falls below a contractually stated amount.

6. Cost of bail-out provision, i.e., do you have the option of accepting higher interest and no bail-out provision or a lower initial interest with a bail-out provision?

7. Interest rate track record for fixed annuities. Investment accounts track records and interest rate track records for variable annuities.

8. Free withdrawal privilege. How much cash can you withdraw from a contract each year without being subject to insurance company-imposed withdrawal charges? Withdrawal from any annuity would be subject to the normal pre-59 1/2 government penalty, currently 10%.

9. Front-end charges. Sales charges applied against initial deposit which reduce your investment.

10. Surrender charges (back-end loads). What percentage of the annuity would be left with the insurance company to cover deferred sales charges if you surrendered the annuity? At what point would such surrender charges no longer exist?

11. Under what circumstances, such as death, disability or an annuity pay-out are the surrender charges waived?

12. Is there market value adjustment? If the annuity contract is surrendered, is the surrender value adjusted as a result of changes in prevailing interest rates? This would be typical of a variable annuity bond account. However, even though it would be atypical, it is found in some "fixed" annuities. You would be wise to avoid the latter.

13. On surrender, may the contract holder recover his investment in the contract in lieu of a cash surrender value if the investment is greater, i.e., you paid more than the contract's current value? Can you choose to take your payments back instead of the cash surrender value?

14. At death, what is the situation for your named beneficiary? With fixed annuities, it would be unusual for the beneficiary to be in a situation where the amount to be paid out was less that the amount invested. However, with variable annuities a significant drop in the stock market could expose an individual to significant principal risk. You will find that with most variable annuities, the beneficiary will receive the annuity at market value or the owner's gross investments in the contract, whichever is greater. You can expect to find approximately a 1/2% charge for this guarantee within the prospectus for the variable annuity. Look for it; it does offer a nice measure of security.

15. Are there any annual fees?

16. What is the commission, and what is its impact on your account?

ranged so that if you are survived by a spouse, the spouse will be allowed to continue the deferred annuity and manage it just as you had during your life. Deferred annuity contracts are not as efficient as single premium life insurance policies in accomplishing the transfer of wealth on to a beneficiary. The annuity contract, while deferring taxation on earnings within the contract until future use, never escapes that pent up income tax liability. If the beneficiary of a qualified annuity contract is not a spouse, those income tax liabilities become the beneficiary's tax liabilities and they will have to be paid as the funds are paid out. That beneficiary that is a non-spouse is not allowed to continue the deferral but must establish a payout arrangement with the insurance company. The income tax liabilities will have to be paid based on the payout arran· gement. Compare this to a life insurance policy in which the death benefit is substantially greater than your investment within the life insurance policy (by the net amount at risk), and the total death benefit is passed to the beneficiary without any income tax liability. The difference in the tax treatment requires you to define your objectives very carefully in order to determine which contract, annuity or life insurance policy will serve you and your family best.

Non-Qualified Annuities—Income Taxation

Non-qualified annuities are contracts that you personally purchase with your after-tax income or capital. Your investment in these contracts constitutes your cost basis. You and/or your beneficiary eventually will get this cost basis back out of your annuity contract without re-taxation. Assuming you do not annuitize an annuity contract—that is, turn it in to a series of payments over a stipulated period of time—periodic withdrawals from these contracts will be considered interest earnings first. When interest earnings have been entirely withdrawn and taxed as ordinary income at the time of withdrawal, the remaining funds (constituting your basis), will be withdrawn and not re-taxed at that time. The exception to this rule is pre-August 14th, 1982 annuity contracts that are taxed in just the opposite fashion. Withdrawals are considered to be principal first, then interest. Annuities are subject to the pre-59 1/2 age penalty tax on withdrawals. The penalty tax will be waived if the owner of the annuity contract is 59 1/2 or older, if he dies, becomes disabled or if the annuity contract is being used relative to the periodic payments required under a personal injury suit. The penalty also will be waived if the benefits are annuitized and paid out as a series of substantially equal payments over the life of the annuitant or over the joint lives of the annuitant and the primary beneficiary.

If you invested in one of these non-qualified annuities prior to August 15, 1982, you may withdraw your cost basis in your annuity contract first. This means that when you withdraw your original investment in that policy it is considered to be your investment first and will not be subject to income taxes or the 10% penalty tax. You will want to make sure that you keep your pre-August 15, 1982 annuity contracts separate from those purchased after that date so that you may continue to take advantage of this ability to withdraw your basis first.

Income taxation of annuity proceeds in the event of the death of an annuitant depend upon whether income has commenced and whether the beneficiary receiving the proceeds of the annuity is the annuitant's spouse. Let us assume that payments have not yet begun and the annuitant dies leaving the proceeds of the annuity to the surviving spouse. The spouse in a qualified plan annuity contract will have the option of continuing the annuity and enjoying continued tax-deferral on earnings if the contract provides for this contingency. On the other hand, if the annuitant has started to receive the benefits and dies leaving the annuity proceeds to the surviving spouse, then the benefits must be distributed at least as rapidly as the method that was in effect at the time of the annuitant's death and taxation will continue to apply to those proceeds. In a non-qualified annuity the spousal beneficiary steps into the shoes of the decendent owner, i.e., continued deferral or continued payout.

If a non-spousal beneficiary receives the proceeds and the annuitant's death occurs prior to distribution of any income, that non-spousal beneficiary may elect a lump sum distribution without penalty but with full taxation on the accrued interest or gain within the contract. Alternatively, the non-spousal beneficiary may elect a series of payments to be made over a period of time not to exceed the beneficiary's life expectancy beginning within one year of the annuitant's death. A non-spousal beneficiary has no option to continue the contract, and the payment is not subject to 10% penalty tax since it is as a result of the annuitant's death. If the annuity income had started prior to the annuitant's death, then the proceeds would have to continue to come out of the annuity at least as rapidly as the method that was in effect before the annuitant's death, with the normal taxation continuing.

The Exclusion Ratio

The taxation of annuitized non-qualified annuity contracts is based upon an exclusion ratio. Since you have directed the insurance company to distribute both principal and interest from the contract in a series of equal periodic payments, the basis (the original after-tax investment in the contract) is paid out as a portion of each of those payments. This portion is determined based on government tables and is not taxed. It often represents 40% to 50% of the total periodic payment being received. This percentage is found by calculating a ratio which is determined by the ratio of your original investment in the contract over what your expected return is in total from your annuity contract. If you outlive the annuity tables, there may come a time when you have received your entire cost basis back from your annuity contract. When that time arrives, all subsequent payments will be subject to ordinary income tax in their entirety. This foolish rule was incorporated in the Tax Reform Act of 1986 and applies to annuities that had not been annuitized as of January 1, 1987. Annuity contracts that had been annuitized before that date enjoy the exclusion ratio for the rest of the annuitant's life and may continue to exclude the same percentage even after the annuitant's entire cost basis has been recovered. The new rule adds an additional income tax burden for senior citizens in their mid-eighties. It would be interesting to learn how much revenue the government expects to receive from this additional tax on senior citizens who have been living on a fixed income for a substantial period of time. Not only has inflation eaten away at their standard of living, but Uncle Sam is now going to increase their taxes also.

Qualified Annuities

Qualified annuities are purchased with funds generated from qualified retirement plans. Contributions to qualified plans generally are not subject to current taxation when they are contributed to the plan. IRAs that qualify for an income tax deduction are qualified plans as are Simplified Employee Pension plans (SEPs), tax-sheltered or tax-deferred annuities-(TSAs), 401(k) plans, profit-sharing plans, pension plans and the like. These qualified plans are unique because in addition to enjoying the deferral on the earnings within the plan that you enjoy within all annuities, you and your employer may also make capital investments into these plans without having to pay taxes on the amount of investment in the year of contribution. Since you have never paid taxes on the amount contributed to the plan, you do not establish a cost basis. In many instances, there is nothing to return to you from the tax deductible qualified plans that is not taxable. All payments from such contracts are subject to ordinary income tax at the time received. These qualified plans are usually among the best investment opportunities available. Even with marginal tax brackets in 1989 as low as they are, the tax advantages of these plans are difficult to surpass. For example, if you are in the 30% marginal tax bracket and you qualify for one of these plans, a $100 contribution would reduce your income taxes by $30. The $30 reduction on your income tax, and a $100 investment into the plan, means that your investment has cost you

$70. At a cost of $70, you will have $100 on your net worth statement. That is a $30 gain on a $70 investment, which translates to a 42.8% rate of return. This return does not even count any actual investment return that your $100 is earning inside of the plan, and that return also is sheltered from current taxation.

Your employer may encourage you to invest in these plans by offering to match, for example, 50% of your contribution. If so, rather than gaining $100 on your net worth statement for a $70 investment, your $100 would appear on the net worth statement along with $50 of your employer's money, giving you a $150 total on your $70 investment, or an $80 gain on a $70 investment. This is a return of 114%. Uncle Sam will do all in his power to prevent you from using these monies indiscriminately prior to age 59 1/2, but they do provide some indirect benefits before that time. A strong net worth statement allows you to pursue more opportunities than does a weak one.

If you would like to retire someday at 100% of your standard of living, you will have to take advantage of social security, your employer's qualified retirement plans and save 20% of your gross income each and every year. It's a tough task. There is no better way to begin this personal accumulation pattern than by participating at the maximum level possible in the employer-provided plan that allows you to invest with pre-tax dollars.

One unique feature of qualified plans is that you are required to begin payouts from these plans, or the annuities that hold the cash in these qualified plans, in the year in which you attain age 70 1/2. With non-qualified annuities, the basic objective is to continue deferral of annuitization as long as possible in order to maintain flexibility and to continue to compound the earnings within the contract without current taxation. The present IRS regulations requiring you to start making withdrawals from all of your qualified plans at age 70 1/2 do not change this basic strategy. In order to comply with Uncle Sam's distribution rules, it is not necessary for you to annuitize your contract. For example, the minimum distribution requirement at age 70 1/2 is 1/16 of your balance on the previous December 31. One-sixteenth is only 6.25% of that balance, and hopefully 6.25% is less than what you are earning within your contract. Thus, even if you pull out the 6.25%, the principal balance on the following December 31 is likely to be higher than it was on the December 31 prior to your 70 1/2 birthday. The next year you will have to withdraw about 7% and by the time you attain age 75, about 8%. As a result, even when you comply with the requirements to take distributions each year after you attain age 70 1/2, you still can maitain your annuity, make the required withdrawals, earn a substantial return not subject to ordinary income tax, and ideally not diminish the principal within your account.

The case is even better for those with qualified plans who elect to make withdrawals from their plans on a joint and last survivor basis because the table for this type of distribution requires an even smaller amount to be distributed. For example, if you are age 70 1/2 and your spouse is age 68, only 4.65% of your account must be withdrawn. In the following year, it would be approximately 4.83% and at age 75, the required distribution amount would be about 5.8%. Not until you are age 85, would the amount required for distribution exceed 10%. Failure to make the required withdrawals will expose you to substantial penalties from Uncle Sam, so make sure you check with your tax advisor and take what you must.

For planning purposes you may use Figure 10–5 if you are making withdrawals on a single basis or Figure 10–6 if you are making withdrawals with a joint beneficiary. Determine the amount in your qualified plan contract or contracts on December 31 of the year preceding the year you reach age 70 1/2. Find the factor based upon your age if based on a single life (Figure 10–5) or based on your own and your joint beneficiary's age (Figure 10–6). Divide the amount in your accounts on the previous December 31 by the factor in the table. That is the minimum amount you must withdraw in that year, all of which will be taxed as ordinary income.

For example, you are a single individual calculating minimum distribution requirements for the year that you attain age 70 1/2. You will find the factor 16 by age 70. This would

Figure 10–5
Ordinary Life Annuities
One Life-Expected Return Multiples

Age	Multiple
70	16.0
75	12.5
80	9.5
85	6.9
90	5.0
95	3.7
100	2.7
115	.5

Figure 10–6
Ordinary Joint Life and Last Survivor Annuities
Two Lives-Expected Return Multiples

	70	72	75	80	85
60	26.2	25.8	25.3	24.8	24.5
65	23.1	22.5	21.8	21.0	20.5
68	21.5	20.8	19.9	18.9	18.3
70	20.6	19.8	18.8	17.6	16.9
73	19.4	18.5	17.3	15.9	15.0
78	18.0	16.9	15.4	13.5	12.3
83	17.1	15.9	14.2	11.9	10.2

mean you must divide your account value on December 31 of the previous year by 16, and take that amount out by April 15 of the following year. If your account value was $100,000 you would have to take out $6,250.00 ($100,000 divided by 16) If you are 70 1/2 and your wife is 68 years old, the factor would be 21.5 and the minimum withdrawal amount would be

$4,625.00 ($100,000 divided by 21.5). If you do wait until after January first of the year following the year in which you attain age 70 1/2 to take a distribution, you will have to take two distributions in that tax year which could increase your income tax liability if the combined withdrawals moved you into a higher tax bracket. The deferral to April fifteenth is available only for the first year distributions. In all succeeding years, distribution must be made within the calendar year. Be cautious in your minimum distribution planning! To take less than the minimum exposes you to a 50% penalty on the amount you should have withdrawn, but did not.

A Rollover IRA Retirement Strategy

The rollover IRA is gaining popularity as a option for the disposition of retirement plan funds. One of the main reasons is because it puts the retiree in control of the funds instead of the ex-employer. It also avoids current income taxation entirely and provides for the continuation of tax-deferred earnings. These funds have been accumulated over a lifetime of work and are likely to be considered core assets that should be managed most carefully.

If you live on only the income from the capital you have in your rollover IRA and never invade principal, you will be better off than if you had annuitized. If you are able to live on less than the income generated within the IRA, you will see your capital increase. This is highly satisfactory not only because you are better off each year, but since your capital base is increasing each year there will be more capital available to generate income. If you are in this happy state of affairs, you may be looking for a way to make reinvested earnings work as hard as they can for you in offsetting the risks of inflation. One way to do this is to dollar cost average the excess earnings from a guaranteed principal guaranteed interest account holding your core assets into one of the common stock accounts in the family of funds available within your rollover IRA contract. This provides for some diversification and, given time and patience, positive investment results. When these earnings become significant, they may be swept back to the safe haven account in which you hold your core assets. This builds up your "safe" account, which then generates more interest that can be used to increase the amounts being dollar cost averaged into the stock account. The more earnings you receive, the more earnings you generate!

Many conservative investors find this a very comfortable method of managing their rollover funds. It enables them to enter the stock market when they would not have been able to do so otherwise, and thereby earn greater returns than they could with compound interest. It increases diversification and allows the retiree to maintain control.

Trading Life Insurance and Annuity Contracts: The 1035 Tax-Free Exchange

Throughout this book we have recommended flexibility as a feature of the life insurance and annuity contracts that you use to enhance your own and your family's financial security. Change is inevitable in everyone's economic situation; if the contract you have purchased is adaptable to your economic circumstances as they change and develop, it is more likely to perform satisfactorily.

You may find yourself owning a life insurance or annuity policy that is no longer suitable. If so, don't just surrender that contract. Income taxes and penalties that may result upon surrender of a contract that will burden you with unnecessary expenses. Section 1035 of the income tax code allows you to make tax-free exchanges of a life insurance policy for another life insurance policy, or a life insurance policy for an annuity contract, or an annuity contract for another annuity contract. You simply trade contracts. However, you cannot trade an annuity contract into a life insurance policy without taxation.

To effect a 1035 tax-free exchange you assign your company A contract to company B and direct company B, in writing, to put the company A contract proceeds into the company B life insurance contract or annuity that you prefer. If done properly, you should not have to pay income taxes on the transaction. You may, however, have to pay surrender charges to company A and acquisition charges to company B. If these are acceptable and the alternative contract is better suited to fulfilling your needs, then proceed.

The advantage of the tax-free exchange is that you will not have to pay any taxes on the gains earned in the original contract at the time of the exchange. What if there are no gains in the original contract? Indeed, what if there is a loss? Surrendering the contract does not allow you to take a deduction for that loss on your income tax return. Losses as a result of surrendering life insurance or annuity contracts are not deductible. The reason you have a loss in the old contract is because your cost basis, your investment, exceeds the capital accumulated in the contract. The advantage of doing a 1035 tax-free exchange in this case is that you would be rolling that high basis into the new contract. The higher the basis in your new contract, the more you will be able to take out of that contract in living benefits without taxation. Old policies that have not performed adequately can still be valuable to you in this way. In short, regardless of the gain or loss in your old contracts, the 1035 tax-free exchange is likely to be to your economic advantage.

The 1035 tax-free exchange is also advantageous if you own a life insurance policy and, at some point in the future, determine that it is no longer needed or appropriate. You can reclaim the money that you have put into your contract (your basis) out of your life insurance policy by making a withdrawal. Then, via a 1035 exchange of that policy into an annuity contract you can avoid current taxation on the gain. From that point forward, the investment return within the contract will not be subject to the mortality charges inherent in a life insurance policy, your tax-deferral will continue and your cost basis in the contract will include all of your previously paid life insurance costs and expenses!

Many old annuity contracts were less flexible and provided lower investment returns to contract holders than do those being issued today. If you find yourself with such a contract, you may opt for a 1035 exchange into an annuity contract that would better suit your present needs and provide you with greater investment returns and more flexibility.

You will note we have not suggested tax-free exchanges from an annuity contract into a life insurance contract, since Section 1035 does not permit that type of tax-free exchange.

Summary

Annuities are not strictly payout vehicles demanding equal periodic payments to an annuitant who stands the risk of forfeiting a substantial amount of his investment to an insurance company if he or she does not live long enough. That situation is easily avoided. Annuities today can be extremely efficient asset accumulation vehicles that will serve you well in retirement. We would suggest that you avoid annuitization until such time as it becomes the only remaining viable economic solution. In contracts, you should look for convenience and flexibility. Examine carefully the expenses in the contract, the contract limitations, the variety of accounts, the service, the reporting, management and, by all means, the company.

ELEVEN

INSURANCE COMPANY, PRODUCT, AND AGENT SELECTION

Prior to the mid-1970's, few financial professionals or consumers worried about the financial integrity of insurance companies. Street talk regarding a company, its products, service and stability would serve as a good enough indicator for most people.

We have learned that such confidence was unjustified. Many readers will remember the Equity Funding fiasco in which insurance company staff people actually manufactured phoney policies for non-existent insureds. The fraud was finally exposed by an alert reporter. Then came the Baldwin-United failure (no relation to the author!), in which the consumer was promised "too good to be true" interest rates and salespeople received "too good to be true" commissions. Many have been shocked that insurance companies can fail, shocked at their failure to provide service, product failures, abandonment of products and, yes, the economic collapse of the company itself. According to an article in *Forbes*, "You Bet Your Life" (July 10, 1989, page 38), insurance companies were failing at the rate of approximately 1 per year for the 20 years prior to 1987 and about 12 per year since 1987. Obviously, company selection is important to your economic health. When you consider that there are 2,265 life insurance companies to choose from in 1989 and 125 of them do 85% of the business, you can understand why a substantial reduction in the number of companies is inevitable.

How do you protect yourself against potential insurance company failures? Deal with only the biggest and the best, those who have been in business for many years. Fortunately there are a number of public sources of information and assistance to help you locate them.

State Regulation

Insurance companies are primarily regulated by the individual states. Assuming the insurance companies that you have chosen are licensed to do business within your resident state, you have that one level of protection. You may assume that your state insurance department has examined the company and its products and found them to be in compliance with state regulations. Unfortunately, this first level of protection isn't always reliable. In spite of state regulations, insurance companies have failed and caused economic harm to their clients. William H. Smythe, Executive Director of the National Association of Insurance Commissioners (NAIC) securities valuation office in New York once said, "We regulators don't have the authority to tell guys how to run their businesses. We almost have to wait for a disaster to happen, when it comes down to it."

The state does, however, collect information about companies doing business within the state that can be of value.

Items such as the company's annual Convention Statements and Schedule M should be available upon request and will give you the information the company is providing to the regulators regarding its financial condition and the assumptions used in their illustrations. If you have a concern about an insurance company, call your state insurance commissioner's office and ask questions. Your call may trigger action that saves you and perhaps someone else from economic harm. So do not be reluctant to make it.

The states vary in the quality and quantity of their regulation. New York State is noted for being the toughest within the industry. Many people say that New York is too conservative and difficult, but a restrictive approach can be an advantage to you as you try to pick an insurance company that will be a survivor in these volatile times. Ask if the company in question is licensed to do business in New York. If it is and it has agreed to follow New York rules wherever they do business, you have the first level of assurance from the New York regulators in addition to those of your own state. A relatively small minority of the two thousand two hundred and sixty-five companies you have to choose from are licensed in New York.

A. M. Best Company

A second source of public information is the A. M. Best Company of Oldewick, New Jersey, the oldest insurance industry rating service. This company provides information regarding an insurance company's financial condition, a synopsis of its history, information on its management, operating commitments, and the states in which it may write business. A. M. Best Company also grants its own ratings to companies, designed to reflect strength and weaknesses in four areas: underwriting, expense control, reserve adequacy, and investments. In most cases you would be wise to place your trust in companies rated A or A+ by Best's. Some critics question the integrity and meaningfulness of the Best ratings, claiming that the information upon which the ratings are based may be too old and that insurance companies have the ability to pressure Best's for better ratings. Best's, of course, vigorously defends its integrity and objectivity. For you, Best's is only one source of information regarding the ability of an insurance company to make good on its promises. A.M. Best Company may be contacted directly at Ambest Road, Oldewick, New Jersey 08858.

Figure 11–1, provided by Best's, shows the meaning of the A.M. Best rating classifications, how they may be modified and how the "not assigned" ratings are to be interpreted. You will find the Best's reports in your local library. Use only the most current book. Many insurance companies and agents also can provide summaries of Best reports regarding the companies they are recommending to you.

Standard and Poors

Standard and Poors has a service which rates a very modest number of companies on their "claims paying ability". Major employers trying to find a source for guaranteed interest contracts for their retirement plans would use this service to evaluate the financial strength of competing insurance companies. An insurance company wishing to be rated by Standard and Poor's Corporation pays about $20,000 to obtain a rating. If the company is dissatisfied with the rating S & P has given them, it has the option of instructing S & P not to publish it. The S & P ratings may be modified by the addition of a plus or minus sign, and are interpreted as shown in Figure 11–2 provided by S&P.

Note that a company could have an A+ rating from S & P and be in the third level of their ratings. You easily could be misled if you assumed that this A+ rating was a Best's top rating. If you use these ratings in your decision making, know what they mean and how they vary.

Standard and Poor's Corporation is located at 25 Broadway, New York, New York 10004. However, these reports generally are not available to the public unless the insurance company which purchased the report chooses to make it available to you. Ask for it.

Figure 11-1
Best's Rating Classifications

A+ (Superior)
Assigned to those companies which in Best's opinion have achieved superior overall performance when compared to the norms of the life/health insurance industry. On a relative basis A+ (Superior) rated insurers generally have demonstrated the strongest ability to meet their respective policyholder and other contractual obligations.

A (Excellent)
Assigned to those companies which in Best's opinion have achieved excellent overall performance when compared to the norms of the life/health insurance industry. On a relative basis A (Excellent) rated insurers generally have demonstrated a strong ability to meet their respective policyholder and other contractual obligations.

B+ (Very Good)
Assigned to those companies which in Best's opinion have achieved very good overall performance when compared to the norms of the life/health insurance industry. On a relative basis B+ (Very Good) rated insurers generally have demonstrated a very good ability to meet their policyholder and other contractual obligations.

B (Good)
Assigned to those companies which in Best's opinion have achieved good overall performance when compared to the norms of the life/health insurance industry. On a relative basis B (Good) rated insurers generally have demonstrated a good ability to meet their policyholder and other contractual obligations.

C+ (Fairly Good)
Assigned to those companies which in Best's opinion have achieved fairly good overall performance when compared to the norms of the life/health insurance industry. On a relative basis C+ (Fairly Good) rated insurers generally have demonstrated a fairly good ability to meet their respective policyholder and other contractual obligations.

C (Fair)
Assigned to those companies which in Best's opinion have achieved fair overall performance when compared to the norms of the life/health insurance industry. On a relative basis C (Fair) rated insurers generally have demonstrated a fair ability to meet their policyholder and other contractual obligations.

Best's Rating Modifiers

The following Rating Modifiers may be assigned to a Best's Rating classification of A+ through C. These modifiers are used to qualify the status of an assigned Rating. The modifier will appear as a lower-case suffix to the rating.

"c"—Contingent Rating. Temporarily assigned to a company when there has been a decline in performance in its profitability, leverage and/or liquidity results, but the decline has not been significant enough to warrant an actual reduction in the company's previously assigned Rating. Best's evaluation may be based on the availability of more current information and/or contingent on the successful execution by management of a program of corrective action.

"e"—Parent Rating. Indicates a company which meets Best's minimum size requirement and is a wholly owned subsidiary of a rated life/health insurer; however, it has not accumulated at least five consecutive years of operating experience for rating purposes. The parent company's Rating is referenced for companies which meet this criteria until such time as the subsidiary is assigned a Best's Rating.

"p"—Pooled Rating. Assigned to companies under common management or ownership which pool 100% of their net business. All premiums, expenses and losses are prorated in accordance with specified percentages that reasonably relate to the distribution of policyholders' surplus of each member of the group. All members participating in the pooling arrangement will be assigned the same Rating and Financial Size Category, based on the consolidated performance of the group.

"r"—Reinsured Rating. Indicates that the Rating and Financial Size Category assigned to the company is that of an affiliated carrier which reinsures 100% of the company's business.

Ratings "Not Assigned" Classification

Companies not receiving a Best's Rating (A+ to C) are assigned to a Rating "Not Assigned" classification (abbreviated NA) which is divided into ten classifications to identify the reasons why the company was not eligible or assigned a Best's Rating. The primary reason is identified by the appropriate numeric suffix.

NA-1 Inactive – Assigned to a company which has no net insurance business in force or is virtually dormant and is not 100% reinsured by another company. For example, Best's normally continues to report on an inactive company if it is associated with a group or is an unaffiliated stock company pending sale to a new owner.

NA-2 Less than Minimum Size – Assigned to a company whose annual net premiums written do not meet Best's minimum size requirement of $1,000,000. Exceptions are: the company is 100% reinsured by a rated company; or is a member of a group participating in a business pooling arrangement; or was formerly assigned a Rating and is expected to meet the minimum size requirement within a reasonable period of time.

NA-3 Insufficient Experience – Assigned to a company which meets Best's minimum size requirement, but has not accumulated at least five consecutive years of representative operating experience. For most companies, the year that Best's anticipates assigning a Rating is referred to in the report on the company as set forth in Best's Insurance Reports, Life/Health Edition. For all life/health companies in this category which are wholly owned subsidiaries of a rated life/health insurer, the Rating of the parent company will also be shown for reference purposes in Best's Insurance reports, Life/Health Edition, until such time as the subsidiary is assigned a Best's Rating.

NA-4 Rating Procedure Inapplicable – Assigned to a company when the nature of its business and/or operations are such that Best's normal Rating procedure for life/health insurers do not properly apply. Those companies writing lines of business uncommon to the life/health field; or companies not soliciting business in the United States; or companies which are not actively soliciting new business and are in a run-off position; or companies whose sole insurance operation is the acceptance of business written directly by a parent, subsidiary or affiliated insurance company; or those writing predominantly property/casualty insurance under a dual charter would be assigned to this classification.

NA-5 Significant Change – Assigned to a previously rated company whose representative operating experience has been or is expected to be significantly interrupted or changed. This may be the result of change in ownership and/or management whereby the existing book of business is sold or reinsured; or a significant revision in the portfolio of coverages offered; or any other relevant event(s) which has or may affect the general trend of a company's operations. Depending on the nature of the change, Best's rating procedure may require a period of from one to five years to elapse before the company is eligible for a rating.

NA-6 Reinsured by Unrated Reinsurer – Assigned to a company which has reinsured a substantial portion of its book of business or maintains considerable amounts of reinsurance recoverable in relation to policyholders' surplus with reinsures which have not been assigned a Best's Rating.

NA-7 Below Minimum Standards – Assigned to a company that meets minimum size and experience requirements, but does not meet the minimum standards for Best's Rating of "C."

NA-8 Incomplete Financial Information – Assigned to a company which fails to submit, prior to the Rating deadline, complete financial information for any year in the current five-year period under review. This requirement also includes all domestic life/health subsidiaries in which the company's ownership exceeds 50%.

NA-9 Company Request – Assigned when a company is eligible for a Rating but disputes the Best's Rating assignment or procedure. If a company subsequently requests a Rating assignment, Best's policy normally requires a minimum period of three years to elapse before the company is eligible for a Rating.

NA-10 Under State Supervision – Assigned when a company is under conservatorship, rehabilitation, receivership or any other form of supervision, control or restraint by state regulatory authorities.

Figure 11–2
Ratings By Standard & Poor's Corporation

AAA Extremely strong capacity to meet contractual policy obligations.

AA A very strong capacity to meet contractual policy obligations.

A Strong capacity to meet contractual policy obligations.

BBB Adequate capacity to meet contractual policy obligations.

BB, B,
CCC Uncertain or weak capacity to meet contractual policy obligations, with 'CCC' assigned to those with the weakest or most uncertain capacity.

D Default. Terms of the obligation will not be met.

These ratings may be modified by the addition of a plus or minus sign to show relative standings within the major rating categories.

Moody's

Moody's concentrates more heavily on the quality of the company's investment portfolio. The Moody's Investor Service ratings shown in Figure 11–3 may be divided into three sub-categories. This company is located at 99 Church Street, New York, New York 10007. Moody's ratings, like S&P's, are not generally available unless the insurance company chooses to make them available to you.

Duff & Phelps

Duff & Phelps (55 East Monroe Street, Chicago, IL 60603) provides an overall approach in its credit ratings and has a reputation of quality and integrity. The Duff & Phelps ratings apply to corporate debt, preferred stock, real estate, asset backed financings and the insurance company's claims-paying ability. Its rating service includes an insurance company management interview, quantitative analysis, and a view of the company's future. The ratings are updated quarterly in an effort to make the material more timely. D&P will rate approximately thirty insurers during the 1989-1990 period as contracted for by the insurance companies. The D&P ratings probably will only be obtainable from the insurance companies that have contracted for their services. The ratings are described in Figure 11–4.

Company Annual Reports

A review of the company's financial statements and annual report also is in order. These annual reports are readily available from each insurance company and you definitely should ask for them. At least read the President's letter. It should help determine what is going well for the company and what is going poorly. Obviously, you want products and services that are doing well because they will receive the resources and attention of the company. Poorly performing products and services are likely to receive less enthusiastic attention or

Figure 11–3
Ratings By Moody's Investors Service

Aaa   Insurance companies which are rated Aaa are judged to be of the best quality. Their policy obligations carry the smallest degree of credit risk. While the financial strength of these companies is likely to change, such changes as can be visualized are most unlikely to impair their fundamentally strong position.

Aa   Insurance companies which are rated Aa are judged to be of high quality by all standards. Together with the Aaa group they comprise what is generally known as high-grade companies. They are rated lower than the best companies because long-term risks appear somewhat larger.

A   Insurance companies which are rated A possess many favorable attributes and are to be considered upper-medium grade. Factors giving security to punctual payment of policyholder obligations are considered adequate but elements may be present which suggest a susceptibility to impairment some time in the future.

Baa   Insurance companies which are rated Baa are considered as medium-grade, i.e., their policyholder obligations are neither highly protected nor poorly secured. Factors giving security to punctual payment of policyholder obligations are considered adequate for the present but certain protective elements may be lacking or may be characteristically unreliable over any great length of time. These companies' policy obligations lack outstanding investment characteristics and in fact have speculative elements as well.

Ba   Insurance companies which are rated Ba are judged to have speculative elements; their future cannot be considered as well assured. Often the ability of these companies to discharge policyholder obligations may be very moderate and thereby not well safeguarded during other good and bad times in the future. Uncertainty of position characterizes policyholder obligations of insurance companies in this class.

B   Policyholder obligations of insurance companies which are rated B generally lack characteristics of the desirable insurance policy. Assurance of punctual payment of policyholder obligations over any long period of time is small.

Caa   Insurance companies which are rated Caa are of poor standing. They may be in default on their policyholder obligations or there may be present elements of danger with respect to punctual payment of policyholder obligations and claims.

Ca   Insurance companies which are rated Ca are speculative in a high degree. Such companies are often in default on their policyholder obligations or have other marked shortcomings.

C   Insurance companies which are rated C are the lowest rated class of insurance companies and can be regarded as having extremely poor prospects of ever attaining real investment standing.

Figure 11–4
Ratings By Duff & Phelps, Inc.

AAA   Highest claims-paying ability. Risk factors are negligible.

AA+,
AA,
AA-   Very high claims-paying ability. Protection factors are strong. Risk is modest, but may vary slightly over time due to economic and/or underwriting conditions.

A+,A,
A-   High claims-paying ability. Protection factors are average and there is an expectation of variability in risk over time due to economic and/or underwriting conditions.

BBB+,
BBB,
BBB-   Below-average claims-paying ability. Protection factors are average. However, there is considerable variability in risk over time due to economic and/or underwriting conditions.

BB+,
BB,
BB-   Uncertain claims-paying ability and less than investment-grade quality. However, the company is deemed likely to meet these obligations when due. Protection factors will vary widely with changes in economic and/or underwriting conditions.

B+,B,
B-   Possessing risk that policyholder and contract holder obligations will not be paid when due. Protection factors will vary widely with changes in economic and underwriting conditions, or company fortunes.

CCC   There is substantial risk that policyholder and contract holder obligations will not be paid when due. Company has been or is likely to be placed under state insurance department supervision.

be cut. Scan the remainder of the report for information pertinent to the sector of the company in which you are interested. Do not miss the footnotes—often the most important warnings appear in footnotes.

Caution

There is one other pamphlet service that you may encounter. It is Standard Analytical Services, of St. Louis, Missouri. It gives a descriptive report of a company relative to the so-called "25 giants" of the life insurance industry. It probably is not accidental that it looks similar to a Best's pamphlet and that it is bought mostly by companies that do not get a top rating from Best's. Professionals question the credibility and usefulness of the Standard Analytical reports.

The bottom line is that you can't know everything. The information you obtain will inevitably be dated. If an insurance company is trying to fool you and the regulators, it is very likely that you will find out too late. For this reason, we continue to advise you to work with the biggest and the best insurance companies, whose primary business is insurance. A company whose primary focus is not insurance will find it very easy to rid itself of an under-performing insurance subsidiary.

If your agent leaves the insurance business you are referred to as an "orphan" until a new agent is assigned to you. If the company you have your policy with is sold or ceases to exist, you also become an orphan. Both situations are likely to be detrimental to your economic health, so choose both agent and company with care.

State Guarantee Funds

There are state guarantee funds for insurance in approximately 39 states. If you are lucky enough to reside in such a state at the time of a loss and, if the state has an adequate guarantee fund at that time, you may benefit. When Baldwin-United (primary business, piano making) failed in 1983, the life insurance industry and regulators worked diligently for five years to contain the damage. Those who owned Baldwin-United contracts endured five years of uncertainty about their investments. They finally did receive a settlement which generally covered the principal they had invested but not the exorbitant interest rates they had been promised. You certainly couldn't say that they did not suffer a loss!

Companies that promise unachievable interest rates take business away from honest companies, and then leave a mess when they fail. Informed taxpayers are objecting to these practices in the banking and savings and loan industries. Eventually, we will see the same reaction in the insurance industry. Responsible insurance companies cannot, and eventually will not, absorb insurance company failures at the expense of their own contract owners and stockholders. You, the consumer, must consider carefully the creditworthiness of the general accounts of the insurance companies into which you are entrusting your funds. In short: don't bet on state guarantee funds, mergers, acquisitions and reorganizations in the insurance industry to bail you out of a failing company.

Joseph M. Belth

Joseph M. Belth, Ph.D., is a professor of insurance at Indiana University and the publisher of a monthly publication called *The Insurance Forum*. He has been referred to as the Ralph Nader of the insurance industry. He exhibits a bulldog-like tenacity in his pursuit of financial information on insurance companies in order to keep consumers and financial professionals informed. He is not the least bit hesitant to point out the companies that he believes are involved in questionable practices. His monthly publication can be obtained by writing to: *The Insurance Forum*, P.O. Box 245, Ellettsville, IN 47429.

Within *The Insurance Forum*, it has been Dr. Belth's practice to publish a list of insurance companies that have received top ratings from the A. M. Best Company for the last ten consecutive years. You may request his most current list by mailing your request along with a stamped, self-addressed envelope to the address above.

Professor Belth is a controversial source of information. He has the courage to express his opinions in no uncertain terms, and consequently many take issue with him. However, he does give the background data that leads him to his conclusions. This helps you understand the issues and risks involved so that you can make more informed purchase decisions.

Product Impact on Company Selection

Another important factor in company selection is the product line offered by the company you are considering. There are some multi-line companies that will provide for both the property and casualty needs of individuals and companies, as well as the life, annuity and health insurance needs. However, it is unusual for one insurance professional to have expertise in all of these fields though there are, of course, exceptions. There are many partnerships of property/casualty and life agents who combine their expertise to serve their clients. Most insurance companies are oriented toward property/casualty or toward life, annuity and health. One rule of thumb to remember is that the company you choose should have a sufficiently diverse product line so that if one of its products is legislated out of existence the company does not fail with it, leaving you "orphaned." Diversification of product provides a degree of safety and flexibility for insurance companies just as it does for individuals.

You want to avoid the risk that the insurance product you select may fail to perform as promised. This can happen not only as the result of insurance company insolvency but also because the product becomes unprofitable and the company decides to divest itself of the unprofitable unit: e.g., "CIGNA Considers Sale of Life Insurance Unit: Analysts said the sale of the unit would improve the company's long term profits and reduce costs." (Reuters, January 7, 1989); "Integrated Resources Life Up for Sale." (*National Underwriter*, September 4, 1989)—and so on.

Company Selection Involves Intermediary Selection

Salespeople can greatly influence product selection and satisfaction. You should learn to distinguish the "client-oriented" salesperson from the "product" salesperson. The product salesperson develops an expertise and an efficient marketing plan for a specific "hot product." Product specialists can be used to your advantage because of their comprehensive knowledge of that specific product. However, it could be to your disadvantage if the "hot product" is sold to you as a solution for a problem you don't have. For example, single premium life is a good product, but it is not appropriate for every client. In 1986-87 it was sold indiscriminately by "hot product" salespeople who marketed it more for their personal wealth enhancement than for that of their clients.

On the other hand, highly technical products such as pension plans, profit-sharing plans, 401(k)s and other qualified plans may be more efficiently handled and serviced by product specialists. Frequently, a client-oriented generalist works jointly with a product specialist to make sure you get adequate service and technical assistance with specialized products.

You need to understand the type of salesperson with whom you are working so that you can determine his role in your risk management process. The choice is yours, but don't think that hiring a qualified, empathetic salesperson is an admission of naiveté. Can you do it alone? If so, can you do it better than if you had hired the proper salesperson? Exactly what would the salesperson cost you?

Know what *you* are paying the salesperson. How much of the money transferred to the insurance company was allocated to pay the salesperson? In these days of contingent deferred sales load products, you often will find that the salesperson receives more commission dollars than are actually subtracted from your funds in the first year. This is because the insurance company advances the pay to the salesperson and plans on recouping this expense from profits on your product over the years you keep your business with the company. If you keep the business with them long enough, for example ten years, it is all recouped and you will be charged no contingent deferred sales charge after that point. However, if you take your business away from them too soon and they are unable to recoup these expenses, they will charge you a contingent deferred sales charge or back-end load. It is really a rather fair and economical way to pay for the services of good salespeople. If you choose to pay salespeople simply because they are persistent rather than helpful, it is a waste and it is nobody's fault but your own. In short: know who you are buying from, what you are paying them, and why.

Front-end loaded products are still prevalent in today's insurance industry. Expenses in the various products vary greatly. Yet consumers and financial advisors still look at ten- and twenty-year projections that distract from what is really important—the initial expenses taken from funds, which limit the amount of money that can go to work for them in the product. Avoid front-end loads to the extent possible and by all means know how much of your money is going to be working for you in the product in the early years. If the company treats you fairly in the early years, they are more likely to treat you just as fairly in the later years. You can check performance by comparing results annually.

Financial journalists like to debate the need for intermediaries. They contend, "Read our magazine or column and you will not have to pay salespeople." Some suggest that you are best served by dealing directly with a company like USAA that markets by direct mail and referral in order to avoid the salesperson's commission. Alternatively, you have the choice of dealing with the no-load or low-load companies that market directly to the public, or in some cases to financial planners who then add an independent charge for acting as your intermediary. Do not be deceived: you pay marketing expenses whether they are incurred by paying commissions to salespeople or by direct mail, high advertising costs or fees to those who find you a product.

If you are going to hire a salesperson or other intermediary, that person should have the education, integrity and expertise to be your staff employee—preferably someone who has special expertise in your area of need. Interview potential salespeople looking for those qualities. There are approximately 400,000 insurance agents eager to serve you, so you needn't give the business to the first one who knocks on your door. Keep in mind that fewer than one third of those 400,000 are even properly licensed to sell you all the products mentioned in this book. If someone makes negative statements about a particular product, make sure it is actually because of the product, rather than just because the salesperson is not licensed to sell it.

Paying for the Product and Service

Understand that you will pay for the sales process. Even if a product is supposedly "no-load" there is a cost to bring that product to your attention, and you pay that cost. No-loads and low-loads typically have substantial marketing costs and can be expected to use advertising more than companies that employ a salesforce. Companies that market to independent agents do so with good products and services and also with high commission promises and loss-leader interest rates they do not intend to maintain. Which is it your independent agent is recommending to you—the superior product or the higher commission product?

Common wisdom used to suggest that you would be better served dealing with a "broker" or independent than you would with a "captive" agent. The former would have access to all products available from all companies to choose from on your behalf while the latter would have access only to those products provided by the company which employed him.

This theory never did work very well because all insurance salespeople, captive or independent, are limited in their capacity to know everything about every product available. Now more than ever they must question the promises made by the product providers and limit their product search to companies they trust.

The distinction between the independent and captive insurance agent is irrelevant when you consider registered products, those that are related to the securities markets and sold with a prospectus. These stock- and bond-based products are provided to a salesperson through a "broker-dealer" or parent organization that screens the products before they are sold. Most broker-dealers insist that their salespeople sell only the securities-based products that they have pre-approved, which means that the salesperson's broker-dealer affiliation limits the products that the salesperson can offer.

We have recommended that you make your first cut based on the financial strength and integrity of the insurance company and your second cut upon making sure that the companies that you have selected offer the products that you want currently plus a diversified portfolio of products available for your future use. The third cut is the agent or intermediary. Interview a number of them. Find out what products they are licensed to sell. Ask them questions about their background, their approach to the business, their present educational credentials and those that they expect to attain in the future. If the agents that you are interviewing are relatively new in the business, find out what backup services are available to them. Ask who they go to for help in a difficult case and if you think you'll be needing them, ask to meet those individuals also.

You will find that financial planners like to have quality insurance professionals available to them. Certified Financial Planners and Chartered Financial Consultants will look for insurance professionals with educational credentials comparable to their own in the insurance field. They will look for a Chartered Life Underwriter (CLU), who has received his designation from the American College in Bryn Mawr, Pennsylvania. CLU's must have completed ten semester courses and ten examinations over approximately a five-year period in order to attain this designation. Certified Financial Planners and Chartered Financial Consultants also have had education in the personal risk management area. If the agent that you are interviewing has taken any of these advanced courses, it indicates two things that are advantageous to you. First, that the individual is committed and capable of taking and passing such exams; second, that he is committed to learning more in order to serve you better. The agent has, in effect, worked to become qualified to serve as your insurance consultant.

When you find a person that meets your requirements, with whom you can communicate and who can obtain the insurance products that you want, it will not matter how you pay that individual for his services. Integrity is not purchased by paying an individual consultant fees rather than commissions. The individual you work with will either have integrity and a professional approach to serve your best interests rather than his own or he will not. It will be up to you to sense the presence or the absence of such integrity. That is why the interview is so important.

The bottom line is that most of us need help in selecting and managing insurance products. We will pay for this help one way or the other. Seek the best qualified help you can find because poorly designed insurance is detrimental to your economic health, whereas properly owned, designed, funded, and managed insurance products are productive and valuable in enhancing your family's financial security.

Once you have found company, product line and intermediary, you are in an excellent position to compare costs and benefits. Our objective at the outset of this book was to give you the tools to manage the products you purchase from insurance companies profitably and efficiently. By now, we hope you are able to do just that. With the tools we have provided herein, you are the new sophisticated consumer. You know the questions to ask and the benefits to demand. You know that when you are offered choices within the various insurance company products, your basic rules of thumb will be to:

1. Know the costs built into the product especially in the early years.
2. Establish long-term relationships with quality insurance companies and quality intermediaries.
3. Choose control over no-control.
4. Choose flexibility over inflexibility.

5. Choose quality over current or future interest rate promises.
6. Choose a survivor among insurance companies and intermediaries.
7. Accept the fact that assets within insurance contracts require your management just as does every other asset on your balance sheet. Vigilance pays.

Life insurance and annuity contracts that are carefully purchased and well-managed are wonderful wealth-building and wealth-preserving vehicles. The basic truth is that you can do almost everything you can do with CDs, stocks, bonds and mutual funds within life insurance and annuity products today and at the same time protect the return on those investments from being diminished by current income taxes.

Summary

The criteria to be examined in selecting insurance companies are: financial strength, longevity and integrity. Therefore, you will want to deal only with companies rated A or A+ by Best, those that are not likely to end up on the cutting room floor because a single product became unprofitable and unimportant. You probably will tend to select from the large household names in insurance that have been in the business for many decades and are likely to survive your lifetime. They should have the products that you need. If you are concerned with your own (or anyone's) ability to substantiate the financial integrity of the insurance company's books, choose *conduit* life insurance and annuity products. In conduit products, the insurance company administers the mortality and expense side of the contract but your investments, rather than being maintained within the general portfolio of the company, are sent to the separate accounts (mutual funds) of your choice maintained by the company for your use with that particular contract. These accounts are not accessible by the general creditors of the company. You can avoid the unknown creditor risks in the general portfolio by accepting the risks in the separate accounts that are spelled out in the prospectus. This situation has been illustrated dramatically by the financial problems of Integrated Resources, which has issued insurance products that use both the separate accounts and the general accounts of the company. The general accounts are subject to some creditor risk, although it is expected to be minor, whereas the separate accounts are not.

Insurance company selection involves using the same research techniques, tempered with good common sense, that you would use in making any other major purchase in your life. You cannot know everything about a company. Formulas don't always work and available information is not always current or reliable. This doesn't mean that you should despair. Many of the people who have been disappointed with product or company performance are the same people who demanded performance beyond what could reasonably be obtained. They bought from the first person or company who, in order to make a sale, told them what they wanted to hear. The results are inevitable—failure to perform. Be a skeptic. If you are offered a product which sounds too good to be true, ask some of your knowledgeable friends or advisors about it. They may not be able to directly refute the claims of the salespeople; however, if it does not pass "the smell test" or if it defies "economic gravity," don't suppose you are getting a special deal because someone loves you.

Finally, when dealing with professional insurance intermediaries, your most effective questions are, "What would you do to solve this problem if you were in my shoes?," "Why?," "How have you handled this need for yourself?," and "Show me!" These questions put a good deal of pressure on the professional, and it is likely that the way in which they are answered will help you judge if the two all-important qualities—personal integrity and empathy—are present. If they are not, do not do business with that intermediary.

INDEX